Before sacrificing his soul to dark forces in the Square Mile, Geraint Anderson was a long-haired hippy and left-wing idealist. His dream of becoming a trinket-selling global traveller was cruelly dashed when his brother got him an interview at a French bank in the City, which would set him on the rocky road to destruction and despair. He is the bestselling author of CITYBOY and the novel JUST BUSINESS, and a regular media commentator on the financial world he once inhabited. He now lives a quiet life, with his wife and family, exploring the planet and doggedly trying to get to grips with surfing.

Praise for Geraint Anderson:

'Engaging, timely and important . . . an effective indictment of the narcissism and decadence of City life' *The Times*

'Reminiscent of John Grisham . . . he has weaved a pacy page-turner' *News of the World*

'His timing couldn't be better . . . London's pernicious financial world reveals itself in all its ugliness' *Daily Mail*

'As a primer to back-stabbing, bullying, drug-taking, gambling, boozing, lap-dancing, this takes some beating' *Evening Standard*

'If you found *The 39 Steps* short of sex and drugs, Geraint Anderson, aka Cityboy, has kindly corrected John Buchan's oversight . . . an affable romp' *Daily Telegraph*

'Excruciatingly candid' *Sunday Times*

'An undeniably slic sness Post*

By Geraint Anderson and available from Headline

Cityboy: Beer and Loathing in the Square Mile
Cityboy: 50 Ways to Survive the Crunch

Just Business
Payback Time

PAYBACK TIME

Geraint Anderson

headline

First published in 2012 by
HEADLINE PUBLISHING GROUP

First published in paperback in 2013 by
HEADLINE PUBLISHING GROUP

1

Cataloguing in Publication Data is available from the British Library

ISBN 978 0 7553 8177 7

Typeset in Hoefler by Avon DataSet Ltd,
Bidford-on-Avon, Warwickshire

Printed and bound by CPI Group (UK) Ltd, Croydon, CR0 4YY

Headline's policy is to use papers that are natural, renewable and
recyclable products and made from wood grown in sustainable forests.
The logging and manufacturing processes are expected to conform
to the environmental regulations of the country of origin.

HEADLINE PUBLISHING GROUP
An Hachette UK Company
338 Euston Road
London NW1 3BH

www.headline.co.uk
www.hachette.co.uk

For Ramona – the sweetest
midget terrorist currently operating
in the South Wales area.

Acknowledgements

Anyone who has read the acknowledgements in *Cityboy* and *Just Business* will know that I've had the good fortune to have spent most of my life surrounded by a bunch of jokers who I traditionally recognise here for unintentionally supplying me with the gags and phrases that pepper my prose. To the list of usual suspects (Razzall, Changus, Uppy 'The Nose', Toby, bald Al etc) I must now add my Ballinskelligs pal Roger Harty and my brother-in-law Craig 'the man on the telly' Kelly.

Big thanks to Martin Fletcher at Headline and my agent Lizzy Kremer from David Higham, who have both consistently provided me with exceedingly judicious advice. I must also express gratitude to my long-suffering copy editor Nancy Webber whose regular exclamation marks remind me that my writing sometimes borders on the absurd (when, of course, it is supposed to be wholeheartedly absurd!). I once again thank Sophie Lodge who not only designed my website www.cityboy.biz but is also, she tells me, a damn fine 'online profile manager' . . . whatever that is.

Finally, and most importantly, I must thank my lovely wife Emma. She has gone through this book several times with her unforgiving red pen, improving it markedly. Not for nothing is she known to friends and family alike as 'The Inspector'. She also had the good grace not to give birth at the same time as this book was being published . . . which makes a nice change.

If you have any thoughts on this book please email them to me at cityboy69@hotmail.co.uk. If you want to follow me on Twitter I'm known as @cityboylondon and if you'd like to become my Facebook pal I'm known as City Boy there.

Shit, if that lot doesn't satisfy my 'online profile manager' nothing will.

Geraint Anderson a.k.a Cityboy

Prologue

The Barbican
Monday, 15 November 2010, 6.45 a.m.

BRIDGET STARED AT THE DRONES scurrying around ten storeys below her. A river of black umbrellas flowing towards the City. Less than a week ago she'd been one of them. But those days were over, for ever. She lifted her weary head and tried to focus on the office block opposite but her eyelids grew heavier with each passing moment. She closed her eyes and felt the driving rain pound the top of her head and pour down her naked body. She didn't feel the biting cold. Instead, she basked in the warm afterglow from the recent hit on her crack pipe.

Suddenly, a blinding flash of lightning shocked her out of her stupor. For a moment she saw her ghostly reflection lit up in the glass-fronted building across the road – a deathly white apparition, legs together, outstretched arms holding on to the frame of the window. Mary Magdalene on a crucifix. The image imprinted itself on her retina and she saw it again when she blinked. A deafening crack of thunder quickly followed.

The storm was so close.

It felt like the end of the world.

Bridget let her eyelids droop again and began swaying gently from side to side. She'd always loved the feeling of rain dripping down her face and on this dark November morning it felt better than ever. Her lips curled into a slight smile and she began to sway faster and faster, in time to the pounding techno that came from within her flat. As her head moved ever more energetically from side to side, one thought kept repeating itself into the addled nothingness: *All I ever wanted was to be a good person . . . all I ever wanted was to be a good person . . .*

It took less than three seconds for her body to hit the ground. The thud was followed by a sharp crack as her head smashed into the tarmac. Everyone on the street froze. Then there were screams. The woman's thin, pale body lay unnaturally, the chest glued to the road, the broken face pointing towards the sky. It lay there motionless. A stream of blood flowed from under her head, mixing with the rainwater and slipping into the nearby drain. Instinctively, people looked up at the high-rise above the body. Light streamed out of the only wide open window in the building. The cream curtains within billowed in the wind.

Two suited men from opposite sides of the street dropped their umbrellas and ran to the body. They were unsure about what they should do and aware that everyone was looking at them. Eventually, one man tentatively placed a trembling forefinger on Bridget's neck. He knew there wouldn't be a pulse even before he'd felt the lifeless artery. He closed his eyes and shook his head. The other man had already called the emergency services on his mobile phone.

The person in the room ten floors up crept away from the window, paused, then walked to the chair and picked up the coat, hat and scarf that lay upon it. The scarf was used to wipe clean one of the champagne flutes as well as the glass table, which was still smeared with lines of cocaine. The figure eased into the coat, pulled on the woolly hat and bunched up the cashmere scarf so that only a pair of bloodshot eyes was visible.

The door closed silently and the figure walked towards the lift.

Part One

'Our national debt is rising rapidly, not least as the consequence of support to the banking system. We shall all be paying for the impact of this crisis on the public finances for a generation . . . to paraphrase a great wartime leader, never in the field of financial endeavour has so much money been owed by so few to so many' – Mervyn King, Governor of the Bank of England, 19 October 2009.

One

The Queen's Legs pub, Bishopsgate
Friday, 12 November, 1.45 p.m. (3 days earlier)

'ONE FOR THE ROAD, BRIDGE?' I asked, knowing full
well what the time-tested response would be.

'And one for the ones we never rode!' she said,
drunkenly raising a finger in the air.

Bridget and I had first heard those immortal words come
out of the toothless mouth of a sozzled Irishman in a spit
and sawdust bar in Dublin over fifteen years before. We
were halfway through a rain-sodden pub crawl during what
was supposed to be a 'romantic weekend'. Unfortunately,
our mutual propensity to get out of it had ensured that it
had quickly degenerated into a liver-destroying 48-hour
Guinness-quaffing bonanza. Little did that dribbling, bleary-
eyed mumbler know that his doubtless oft-repeated gag had
become a set response within a small circle of Cambridge
pals. Towards the end of every serious drinking session at

least one of us would invariably shout it, usually employing an appalling Irish accent, whilst raising a single, triumphant digit in the air. Nowadays, we all still uttered it occasionally though it merely felt like a desperate attempt to reassert our shared history . . . a faltering reminder of how close we had all once been.

But that wasn't true with Bridget. Of all our Cambridge set, she was my favourite. She always had been. Our relationship during our second year at college had been a torrid, drug-fuelled affair. Outdoor sex in Grantchester Meadows, breaking into King's College Chapel for illicit naked encounters and terrifying come-down arguments that woke up the whole house. There is no doubt she was my first true love, though I know I wasn't hers. Eventually my immaturity had revealed itself and a pointless drunken shag with some dozy fresher had resulted in the relationship's premature end. It had taken me many years to get over Bridget . . . and apart from a three-year relationship with a wonderful girl called Gemma that I also managed to screw up, I had not found anyone like her in the two decades – almost – that had passed since we'd first met. Still, we had managed to remain great friends and even better drinking partners.

She'd hardly aged since those days and the combination of thick auburn hair, pale freckly skin, feline green eyes and her slender, naturally athletic body turned heads wherever she went – both those of lustful men and the even more obsessive ones of jealous women. But it wasn't only her looks that made her so easy to fall in love with; underneath her carefully constructed air of self-assurance lay a shy, insecure girl who made you want to look after her. Within her lay a deep well of melancholy that I, and many others, hoped to rid her of. Her parents' messy divorce during her early teens had chipped away at her confidence, but only those lucky enough to get close to her ever saw the underlying vulnerability that she hid so well. That desperate neediness was surely why she'd ended up with Fergus. If ever a girl needed the strong silent type it was most definitely Bridget. He provided her with the ballast her chaotic life required and she knew he would never leave her or be unfaithful. He was her rock – something I could never be . . . never hope to be. They had got together a year before and although it had taken about six months for me to get used to the idea of Bridge hooking up with my best friend everything was just about OK now. There was no doubt they complemented each other perfectly and had forged a great relationship that looked destined to go all the way. I was happy for them both . . . or at least I kept telling myself that I was.

I returned to our dingy table in a dark, cosy alcove at the back of the pub, shakily trying to balance two pints of Stella without spilling a drop. This had always been our favourite spot – hidden from the prying eyes and gossipy ears that populate the Square Mile. Here we wouldn't be disturbed by some officious little tosser from our bank or a tedious client whose rancid arse we'd be obliged to wrap our lips around. We could have our traditional Friday lunchtime session in this cubbyhole safe in the knowledge that when we stumbled back to the office half-cut there was little chance that some bonus-hungry snitch on the trading floor would be able to contradict our story that we'd been out separately entertaining different clients.

By the time I'd settled myself in my seat Bridget had downed almost a third of her pint. She slammed it on the table and wiped the froth from her mouth with her forearm.

'Erm, reassuringly fucking expensive!' she laughed, mimicking the ubiquitous Stella adverts from a decade before.

Bridget somehow managed to combine being an Olympian deity with behaviour more befitting an East End docker. I'd lost count of the number of times I'd seen a look of bewilderment cross the face of some chinless stockbroker who, on trying to woo her at some awful City bar, had encountered language the bog cleaners at a greyhound track would find filthy. In a client situation she could turn on the charm with the best of them, but when she was relaxed her natural, punchy self emerged like a champion boxer who'd shuffled off his silk gown. Like me, she was a general salesman at Geldlust Bank. I had started there first and, when I heard that we were looking for new brokers, had persuaded the head of sales to interview her. She'd been working for several years at some two-bit French outfit and I knew she would get the job as soon as she sashayed through our door. Once the traders had found out that her surname was Von Blixen – harking back to the distant Dutch heritage that accounted for her height and angular looks – she had immediately become known as the Blonde Vixen – a moniker that amused her despite its blatant inaccuracy. She and I spent our days calling fund managers at large institutions pretending we knew which shares would go up and which would go down. Both of us were highly competent boozers and we'd sometimes take out shared clients together on debilitating 'champers and sniff' sessions that would invariably help bring business to our esteemed bank. Those wide-eyed Thursday nights careering around the West End were my favourite part of a job I'd long since grown to despise but Bridget still seemed to love.

She and I were a good team . . . we'd always been a good team.

This was our fourth pint and I was beginning to feel a little wobbly. Bridget had been matching me drink for drink and had told me several times that I needed to 'strap a fucking pair on'. Each time she said something like that, a few fellow lunchtime drinkers would look round and stare in disbelief at the delicate beauty who had once again spoken so crudely. But Bridget hardly seemed to notice the quizzical glances that were thrown her way. She was on fire that afternoon and nothing was going to come between her and grinning incoherence. When I had earlier suggested a mid-session glass of water to help keep us hydrated she had looked at me with total disdain and exclaimed: 'For God's sake, Steve, you know I never mix my drinks!' I'd heard that line a few hundred times before too. At about two o'clock

Bridget shouted to the bemused barman that he should 'keep 'em coming till I say stop!' and I resigned myself to a serious Friday lunchtime booze-up.

But this was no bad thing because Bridget had been off form for several weeks. She hadn't been drinking and, much to Fergus's delight, hadn't been hoovering up the nozbert as was her wont. She also hadn't been her usual chatty self with me and had even taken off the early part of the week claiming to be 'coming down with something'. I hadn't bought that horseshit for a New York second because she had the constitution of a prize bull and, apart from appearing edgier than normal over the previous few days, had shown no indications of illness. Still, it was great to see her out and about . . . though there was clearly something on her mind. I had sensed throughout the session that she'd wanted to tell me something, but she had so far declined to do so. There had been an underlying nervousness about everything she did. After taking another hefty gulp from my pint I decided to lighten the mood.

'So, how's John?' I asked. 'Still living in that hovel with only tear-stained wank tissues for company?' John Roberts had been a kind of mascot for us at Cambridge – someone we were all very protective of. He'd waltzed in aged sixteen as one of those planet-brained child prodigy freaks that Oxbridge tends to attract. We had taken him under our wing and enjoyed his often unintentionally amusing asides. His social skills were on a par with Rain Man's and to say he wasn't a hit with the ladies would be like saying Harold

Shipman could improve his care for the elderly. He had been viciously bullied at Eton by a bunch of lumbering toffs and was painfully shy. He was a genius but his gift had come at a high price – living in a strange world that no one else seemed to inhabit. He was probably autistic, or at the very least Asperger's, which made him an ideal fund manager, though it had certainly impeded his ascent up the City hierarchy. Hence, he toiled away at a sleepy mutual waiting for a career break that never came. He lived on his own in a poky little flat in Camden where he spent his time obsessively writing lists, nervously pulling out the few remaining hairs on his skinny cranium or glued to youjizz.com . . . literally, by all accounts.

Bridget smirked a little but didn't roll her head back and laugh in the unselfconscious way that had helped make me fall in love with her so many years before. Her polite, half-hearted giggle ended prematurely and her expression suddenly turned serious.

'Well . . . actually he's been acting a bit weird recently. He . . .' She paused for a second and lowered her head. 'He's been kind of . . . stalking me a bit.' Bridget rarely hesitated when she spoke. This had obviously freaked her out.

'What the fuck? I always thought he was gay or asexual or something.'

'Well . . . I've been feeling recently that someone's been following me. I initially dismissed it as coke paranoia but I kept on catching sight of this figure behind me . . . but he was usually a long way away and his face was always hidden by a hat or a scarf. Anyway, a few days ago I thought I saw the same fucker behind me again and this time I waited round a corner and confronted him. I couldn't fucking believe it! It was John! Well, he claimed that it hadn't been him following me around but it had to be, right?' Bridget took a deep breath. 'So, we went to a bar and had a bit of a heart to heart and . . . out of the blue he suddenly tells me that he's in love with me and always has been! Unbelievable, I know! It was kind of sweet but it was also kind of creepy. He seemed resentful of Fergus and I sensed this real anger in him . . . but it's all so bloody repressed. That's what Eton does to you, I suppose. He kept clenching his fists in that way he does, and when I mentioned Colum he looked furious. You gotta tell that arsehole to cut him a bit of slack, OK?'

I wearily nodded my agreement. Colum, our brash, cruel Cambridge mate who had become a star hedge fund manager, loved nothing more than ripping it out of us all, but it was always poor John who received the lion's share of his relentless mockery.

After a long sigh Bridget continued: 'Anyway, I told him I loved him as a friend but that I was in a relationship with Fergus. I think it's all fine now . . . and I just hope he's gone back to doing his karate and bashing his bishop!' She gave a nervous smirk. She was no drama queen and the encounter had clearly rattled her. Her façade of indestructibility had momentarily disappeared.

'Would you fucking credit it? I need to take that young

man out on the razzle ASAP . . . he's obviously spending way too much time on his own. He *is* full of surprises.' My drunkenness was adding to my astonishment. I simply couldn't believe that little old John had had the balls to tell Bridget what he felt . . . something I could never dream of doing. Frankly I could hardly believe that he was even capable of such feelings; it was like hearing that R2-D2 was a serial philanderer.

'That's not the only thing . . . he's taken up dealing again. Nozz-up, beans – the full Monty this time. Only for friends and family, but still, it seems a bit risky at thirty-five. Isn't he too old for that shit? Needs to do something to supplement that meagre fund manager salary, I reckon!' said Bridget, her mood noticeably lightening.

'Christ, I hate to think what a lad with his taste for pharmaceuticals is going to do constantly surrounded by Class A's. His flat's gonna be a twenty-four-hour narc-fest. Shit, next time I'm in church I'll light a candle for his poor septum!' I said, barely concealing my amusement. John had dealt a bit of puff off and on since university, but now he was punting the hard stuff. Compared to the rest of us City highflyers he earned a pittance – that's to say probably only three or four times what a nurse or teacher made for slogging their guts out – so he'd clearly decided to make some money on the side. John had always resented our vast bonuses but had lacked the capacity for the endless schmoozing and non-stop brown-nosing necessary to make it as a stockbroker.

Geraint Anderson

'Anyway,' Bridget said with a conspiratorial smile, her hand furtively placing something on my knee, 'I'm pleased to say this woeful tale has a happy ending . . . here's a wrap of Peru's finest dancing dust. Why don't you hit the gents? Your nose looks like it needs powdering!'

I didn't need another invitation. Five pints of wifebeater always makes this kind of decision-making incredibly easy – like offering a steaming Lancashire hotpot to a starving northerner. I had a few minor qualms about being naughty on a school day but a quick mental check that I had, as usual, left Friday afternoon free of meetings meant that I was quick-marching towards the bogs almost before Bridget had finished speaking. As I bent down in the cubicle and felt the surprisingly decent kuffer slam into my parched sinuses I reminded myself to contact John ASAP – to chat about some important issues, maybe help get him out and about . . . and that kind of thing.

After Bridget's return from her own nasal examination the now highly animated conversation veered, as usual, to the other members of our Cambridge gang, who had been brought together during the first term by a shared love of partying and a disdain for hard work. We constantly hung out with each other to the exclusion of nearly all the other acquaintances we'd made, and the group was cemented after I had got together with Bridget and Rachel had been wooed by Colum. The gang consisted of six characters, most of whom now found themselves working in the Square Mile, which was the destination of choice for Oxbridge leavers in the mid-90s. Anyone who had two brain cells to rub together had been fully aware that the gravy train was starting up and no one had wanted to be left behind on the station watching their peers chug off to the land of milk and honey.

Of the six of our once inseparable group there was only one who was not working in the City: Bridget's boyfriend Fergus Callahan, who had been my best mate both at school and at university. After a brief stint in the army he now toiled away as a financial journalist on the *Guardian* where he had gained a reputation as a righteous, left-wing investigator with a lifelong mission to expose City malpractice and corruption. Fergus and I had been great pals at school and our friendship had grown stronger over the years. He was inscrutable, serious and didn't do small talk, but once you had become his friend you felt in a privileged position. We had seen each other through many scrapes and he had always been there for me during tough times. Whilst he was not one to show his emotions openly he clearly loved Bridget with an enviable passion.

The remaining members of our City cabal were Rachel, Colum and me. Rachel Maguire was the only married one amongst us and had even had the temerity to produce two children. At Cambridge she had loved to remind us that she was an impoverished commoner from up north although she came, in fact, from Altrincham which was, I later found out, a posh suburb of Manchester full of doctors and lawyers. She was much prettier than she believed and although she had become more reserved over the years and less likely to feature on our raucous nights out she could still tell a great yarn after a few drinks. She had a real warmth to her and also a wild side that nowadays revealed itself much less frequently than it used to. Rachel had worked as an equity analyst at Geldlust for several years before being fired two years ago and now earned a relative pittance working at the City regulator, the Financial Services Authority – a poacher turned gamekeeper in the truest sense. She had had a good portion of her fragile confidence knocked out of her by a troupe of bitchy Sloanes at the posh boarding school her parents had banished her to, and a completely dysfunctional relationship with some pencil-necked prick at Cambridge had further damaged her self-esteem. After splitting up with that particular arsehole she seemed to have entered some unspoken competition to go out with as many wankers as possible. Every time she introduced some new beau to our group eyebrows would be raised and bets taken as to how long this particular misfit would last. I didn't get on with the debilitatingly dull man who eventually became her husband and nor, I suspected, did she. She could still be fun but ten years of marriage to a grey accountant and a life revolving around Wimbledon Village had, understandably, taken its toll on her *joie de vivre*.

Colum 'every hole's a goal' Boyd aka Gollum aka 'the unacceptable face of capitalism' was the real star of the show – a chubby, whore-mongering disease-riddled degenerate whose lack of morals was rivalled only by his dearth of scruples. He suffered from an acute case of coke-bloat and his Pillsbury Doughboy complexion and permanently raw nostrils revealed to anyone within a twenty-foot radius his long-standing relationship with the white lady. He smoked almost continuously and boozed seemingly without cessation. He sought out excess in everything – especially in the fields of drugs, money and sex, which he referred to as the Holy Trinity. He had been nicknamed Gollum early on in his life by a perceptive Lord of the Rings fan and had grown to cherish the moniker. On seeing a wrap of coke he'd rub his hands and hiss, 'My precious . . . my precious, we wants it, we needs it,' and after a few drinks he also loved to shout 'The ring is king, long live the ring', which was not actually a reference to some magical artefact but rather his oft-publicly declared enjoyment of anal sex. He was also the very proud owner of an impressive Johnson which he would invariably take out during social gatherings, most notably during Rachel's wedding. He would plop his 'weapon of mass seduction', as he called it, on the head of some seated lady and howl with laughter when she reached up to find out what was weighing down her cranium. He loved chatting about his 'schlong' and would invariably mock those around him for merely having a 'schlort' – especially poor John. He called his chopper Brutus and claimed that its elephantine girth was legendary across four continents. I have no reason to believe he was lying.

If there was anyone in the group whose friendship had long since passed its sell-by date then it was Colum. He may have been sharp, amusing and 'fun' but few more crude, egotistical sociopaths have ever walked on God's sweet earth. Of course, fifteen years as a highly successful hedge fund manager had simply taken all his offensive character traits and multiplied them exponentially, and he now exhibited less charm than a shit-stained bog brush in a Mexican latrine. It was our shared history, pure and simple, that explained his continued role in our lives.

That only left me – Steve Jones, a general salesman at Geldlust, a mid-tier German bank, fourteen years into a debilitating career I'd promised myself would only last five. A gap-year hippy who'd somehow lost his way and ended up 'working for the man'. An old-school graver who vainly hoped that his charm concealed his addictions . . . a pyrrhic victory of style over substance abuse.

My banking career to date had been eminently predictable for a Cambridge graduate keen to make a fast buck. I'd had a bit of trouble a few years back and had had to leave the City for a while, but now I was back milking the system for all it was worth by doing a job that had long ceased to interest me. Prior to my unplanned trip abroad I'd been an equity analyst, but soon after my return I'd become a general salesman – a role that numerous clients had told me I was far better suited to thanks to my prodigious drinking abilities. Bullshitting fund managers over a lobster thermidor or whilst ogling some young Estonian chick's camel toes proved to be eminently preferable to sitting around on my hairy arse calculating the cash flow generated by some dull company's probably unethical Middle Eastern operations.

When not talking codshit to FMs I partied hard and trawled the bars and clubs of London's East End trying and failing to find someone like Bridget. We Cambridge pals met up fairly regularly on a one-to-one basis but the times when the whole gang partied together were becoming few and far between. Rachel's family commitments, John's antipathy towards Colum and Fergus's increasingly sensible behaviour made sure of that. If truth be told, I was alone and unhappy.

Bridget and I stayed for two more hastily consumed pints with the only other noteworthy bit of gossip being the news that Rachel and her John Major-like husband were having a real rocky patch and participating in 'couples therapy'. Bridget described their marriage as characterised by 'mutual suspicion, seething resentment and barely concealed contempt' – words that could have accurately described most of my relationships over the previous decade. I was a little surprised, but not wholly shocked, by this revelation.

We staggered back to the office at around 3.45 p.m. being sure to leave a gap of five minutes between Bridget's return and my own. Both of us had chewed four Trebor Extra Strong mints, essential post-prandial breath concealment kit for any aspiring broker, as my first City guru had explained, on the walk home. By the time we reached Geldlust's impressive atrium any passing colleague would have thought we'd been bathing in mouthwash for hours, such was our pungent aroma. If our bloodshot eyes and unsteady footing hadn't made them suspect we'd spent the afternoon boozing like Scousers on a day trip to Blackpool then the overpowering smell of mint would surely have convinced them.

I took the lift to the eighth floor and, after an immensely satisfying slash, walked through the glass doors and into the cavernous trading floor. I immediately felt my coked-up heart notch up a gear. I was entering the arena ill-prepared. Before me lay an open-plan office the size of a football pitch buzzing with loud conversations and the sound of money being made. Diligent buffoons gazed at myriad computer screens whilst others typed frantically or shouted into telephones. Numerous rows of desks lay between me and my chair and I prayed I'd manage to make my way there without some snide comment from one of the numerous barrow-boy traders who lay between me and my goal. Unfortunately, walking in a straight line was proving troublesome. I locked in on my desk and focused on putting one foot in front of the other, looking directly ahead to avoid any chance of catching my colleagues' prying eyes. Hundreds of salespeople and traders sat around chatting up their clients. Some leant back in their chairs with their feet on the desk in front of them. Occasionally a trader would shout out some obscure nonsense that only the other traders understood. The TV sets suspended from the ceiling playing CNBC and Bloomberg Television on low volume let out a constant stream of barely audible financial gibberish. The odd paper ball flew by and some small groups of people sat around chatting, probably discussing their expectations for the upcoming bonus round. Somehow, after a degree of focus that impressed even me, I made it to my chair without interruption. I wiped the beads of toxic sweat from my forehead, closed my eyes and praised the Lord that I had managed to run the gauntlet successfully.

As I settled down into my chair I looked around to Bridget's desk.

She wasn't there.

Two

Geldlust Investment Bank, the office of the
head of sales
Friday, 12 November, 3.55 p.m.

'LISTEN, YOU NASTY LITTLE FUCKER!' I know exactly
what you're up to. Don't think you're going to get
away with this, you fucking *prick*!' Bridget's usually
beautiful face had contorted itself into a ferocious snarl. The
industrial-strength gak and six pints of strong lager were
certainly making their presence felt. The purple veins in her
temple were standing out against her pale skin. Even taking
into account what she'd just heard in her boss's office that
kind of language was definitely not called for. But Bridget
was in no mood to be calm and collected. The dogs of war
had been unleashed.

'Look, Bridget, rules are rules. During a random check of
your emails by Compliance we have discovered a blatant
infringement of FSA regulations. We have irrefutable proof

of front-running and not to act would mean that we ourselves would be in breach of banking regulations. Our own banking licence would be at risk.' The head of sales, Chris Browning, was trying his best to remain calm despite the relentless onslaught. His usual mask of condescending pomposity was being tested by the fury that was being directed his way. He was used to sweaty-palmed deference, especially at this time of year when bonuses were being calculated, not unremitting abuse, and whilst telling someone they were fired was never likely to be greeted with flowers and chocolates this was something else.

'I'm afraid, Miss Von Blixen, that Mr Browning has no choice here. This is not a witch hunt or a conspiracy. Your email of the third of November to your client Colum Boyd of Alpha Max Capital is a clear case of front-running and it is now out of our hands. The FSA, as is necessary, has already been informed.' The director of Compliance, Diane Bolton, could hardly disguise the pleasure she was taking from the whole episode. Although she had maintained an air of forced friendliness throughout the proceedings, Bridget could sense a smug satisfaction in her every utterance. Miss Bolton, commonly referred to as the Beast of Bodmin by the wags on the trading floor, was probably the least popular person in the whole building. This was not surprising, since it was her job to clamp down on all Geldlust's stockbrokers' favourite ways of making money: insider trading, market manipulation and the spreading of false rumours – which were, of course, the only tried and tested means to bring in guaranteed profits. But Diane's relationship with Bridget had always been especially strained. The fact that she resembled Ann Widdecombe's less attractive sister, complete with a warty chin you could open a can of tinned fruit with, whilst Bridget was a stunning broker who earned four times her salary probably hadn't helped matters.

'Let me see this fucking email,' Bridget sneered through gritted teeth. She could feel her rage bubbling up uncontrollably. She knew she had to restrain herself or she'd do something she regretted, but she felt like picking up Chris's pearl-handled paper knife, jumping over the desk and viciously attacking them both. Diane nervously handed her a single piece of A4, her trembling hand betraying the fact that she wasn't as calm as she wanted to appear.

From: ███████████ @hotmail.co.uk
Sent: 3 November 2010 15:24:35
To: biggun007@gmail.com

Hiya darling,

How's your head feeling on this fine Monday morning?

Are you crying into your cornflakes? Blimey, that moose I left you with looked like someone had set her face on fire and put it out with a shovel! What were you up to? That was scraping the barrel – even for you!

Anyway, here's a little tip from your ever-faithful servant. Grab a few shares of Medicare Industries. It's a $4bn market cap piece of shit pharmaceutical company but who cares? The dickhead analyst over here, Toby Smythe, is about to change his recommendation from Sell to Buy with a 95p price target on Wednesday. That's 40% upside for Chrissakes! Apparently, he had a nice cosy chat with the FD over a few bottles of Moët and the half-year numbers are going to be over 20% above consensus. Toby may be a pile of knob cheese but the clients rate him and you know that a radical opinion change like this *always* moves the market. The shares aren't that liquid so even a little buying will send it sky-rocketing. Fill your boots now (through me of course!), sell on Friday after the press have picked up on it, and everyone's a winner.

Hugs and kisses (but not until you've had a check-up!),

Bxx

There it was in black and white. Bridget recalled sending the email after a boozy, coke-fuelled client lunch at Coq d'Argent that had ended up at the Shoreditch strip joint Browns. She was one of the few female brokers who actively encouraged her clients to go to titty bars and she did it because she knew that it helped 'win friends and influence people'. The male clients she took to what was known as the Pubic Triangle (the confluence of three popular strip joints: Browns, Metropolis and the Sports Bar) would invariably see her as one of the lads and not one of those 'bean-flicking feminist types' who foolishly felt that women exposing their shaven genitalia to leering degenerates for money was somehow degrading. She would sit there like a Greek goddess in a cheap knocking shop, placing pound coins for her clients in the pint pot that was passed around, somehow unaffected by the sleaze that surrounded her. She didn't enjoy it but neither did she especially disapprove of it. It was just the way of the world. The women were simply using the gifts that God has bestowed upon them to make a living. It was not so different from what she did, selling an asset to pinstriped buffoons, though their job looked more fun and less duplicitous. The transaction they offered to the lonely men in the audience was simple: if cash were revealed, so would flesh be. Bridget sometimes wondered if she could do what these women did. She might have been getting on a bit but she had the body for it and knew how to shake a leg when the spirit took her. If that tosser Chris Browning had his way, she thought, it might be the only career option left to her. She had no qualifications and had only ever worked as a stockbroker. Bridget almost smiled to herself as she contemplated her potential new life as a stripper.

Of course, she would never have sent such an email if she had been straight. Informing a market participant of any upcoming potentially price-sensitive analyst's note was a clear breach of regulations. All such information had to be disseminated to the market at the same time otherwise it favoured one client over all the other mugs out there. There were supposed be to 'Chinese Walls' between salesmen and analysts to prevent this type of thing from happening but, as the traders liked to joke, those walls were full of chinks. Brokers at every bank were very adept at finding out when recommendation changes were in the offing so they could inform their closest clients before the note was released. It was a great way of making their high-paying customers a quick buck and, in so doing, getting them on side, but it was always done via a hasty conversation on the mobile or a fireside chat. Bridget knew that all phone calls from the office were monitored and that occasionally work emails were checked. What she hadn't realised was that her personal hotmail account could also be scrutinised. This was the only time she'd made such a slip-up during her five-year career at Geldlust and it seemed to her horribly unjust that she should be called up for it. She pretended to continue reading the email long after she'd reached the final sentence, desperately racking her buzzing cerebellum for an adequate response. She was feeling her world slip away into nothingness.

'Look,' there was a forced calmness to her words, 'I may have fucked up here but you know and I know that we all do this now and again. This is my first screw-up ever and you choose this time to take action? I'm sorry, but if you check the emails of every one of the arseholes on my desk you'll discover something similar if you look hard enough. Loads of people on the first floor have just received a gentle slap on the wrist for this kind of thing. Why are you shafting me?' Bridget hoped that her hard-nosed adversaries would pick up on the veiled threat to Geldlust and its dodgy practices. Geldlust was notorious as one of the most crooked banks in the Square Mile, which was quite an achievement considering the competition. The FSA had come sniffing around on numerous occasions but had so far merely doled out a few paltry fines. Such was Geldlust's semi-criminal reputation that hedge funds who shared a similar laissez-faire perspective would naturally gravitate towards it. A cursory glance at Geldlust's top commission generators revealed a client base of such degenerate tendencies and loose morals that paedophiles, traffic wardens and even *News of the World* journalists would think twice before entering a lift with them.

'If you are insinuating that front-running is standard practice at Geldlust then I'm afraid you're sorely mistaken. We do check all your colleagues' emails and their phone calls and none of them are involved in anything like this,' stuttered Chris, almost convincing himself that he was telling the truth. Suddenly Bridget exploded. She couldn't take any more of this odious horse shit. It was time to bring out the big guns.

'Listen, Chris, I know *exactly* what's going on here. I'm not a *fucking* idiot so *please* don't treat me like one. It's coming up to bonus time, we've had a bit of a shit year and some ageing spunkbucket upstairs has told you to rid yourself of a few brokers so the firm's meagre bonus pool can be spread around fewer people – we've all seen it happen every Christmas every *fucking* year. I've also no doubt that when you were deciding where the axe should fall, the fact that I'm a woman the wrong side of thirty-five who might go off and procreate at any moment meant that I was the logical choice. Paid maternity leave never did much good for the bottom line, eh? You've probably trawled through every *fucking* phone call I've ever made and every email I've ever written hoping to find an excuse to fire me. This is a *fucking* set-up!' The wallop flowing through her veins was making her tirade all the more vitriolic. Bridget was clearly readying herself for a fight and her adversaries were in no doubt that she meant business. After a long pause, a now deeply scarlet Chris spoke up.

'Well, I'm sorry you feel that way. But I'm afraid you simply don't have a leg to stand on,' he said, a triumphant sneer glued to his face. Each further reminder of Chris's misplaced self-belief rendered Bridget more livid, as did her realisation that he was probably right. Front-running might have been standard practice at Geldlust but it was she who had been foolish enough to get caught. Her fellow brokers all had their snouts in the trough but Bridget knew that it was she who was headed to the knackers' yard and no amount of screaming was going to change that. Still, she wasn't in a reasonable mood and it felt good to get some long-harboured feelings off her chest. She'd go down fighting tooth and nail . . . she'd die with her Manolo Blahnik boots on.

'And, of course, this dismissal falls under the category of "gross misconduct" which means I won't get any of the equity I've accrued over the last three fucking years.' A third of every bonus Bridget had received over the previous three years had been squirrelled away by Geldlust in the form of shares and options that she'd only be granted after a five-year period. Bridget had quickly worked out that her dismissal meant that she was not only going to forgo an upcoming bonus she'd estimated would come in at around £400,000; she'd also lose around £350,000 that she'd already mentally banked. That fillip for the bonus pool would now almost certainly be going to some pointless pinheads who'd recently joined on some outrageously generous guaranteed packages.

Bridget had long been aware of the inherent sexism that ran through Geldlust like a crass message through a stick of Brighton rock but she had always considered it a fairly harmless occupational hazard present in all investment banks. Whilst it had not had a dramatic influence on her working life, other than the fact that she'd consistently received bonuses perhaps 20 to 30 per cent lower than no more productive male colleagues', she had chosen to not kick up a fuss. She now wished that she had written down the details and dates of the numerous examples of sexual harassment she'd been subject to whilst working at Geldlust. They could have been very handy at this juncture.

'Well . . . yes . . . I'm afraid that is company policy . . . and again, I'm sorry to say that it's out of our hands,' said the Beast of Bodmin, her upturned lips barely concealing her delight in the displeasure that each new misfortune caused the increasingly irate Bridget.

'Christ, you malicious *tossers*! You do also realise that there's no way in hell any other bank will employ someone who's been fired like this? You do realise I'll never work as a broker again? I won't ever be deemed a fit and proper *fucking* person by the FSA. I love this job. I've given my heart and soul to this fucking company . . . and you jumped-up fuckwits sit there and take away everything that gets me up in the morning! I've scraped things off my shoe that have more humanity than you . . . you sweaty little . . . *piss flaps!*' Bridget herself was somewhat taken aback by the inventiveness of her childish curse, but not half as much as its bewildered recipients. After a long pause Chris spoke again.

'Listen, this is a completely legitimate dismissal. Our lawyers have been through it all with a fine-tooth comb and our case is watertight. Perhaps you should have thought about the consequences of your actions before you decided to so flagrantly break FSA rules. I'm sorry, Bridget, but you made your bed so now sleep in it.' Chris was beginning to play the bad cop too.

Bridget could barely contain her wrath. She found herself looking around for something to throw at her two assailants. But instead of random violence she took a deep breath, made an about turn and marched out of the office. Some sensible part of her booze-addled brain knew that she was high as a kite and needed to restrain herself. If she'd allowed herself to give in to her instincts and do what she really felt like doing she'd be facing a life sentence at Wormwood Scrubs before the year was out. Before slamming the door so hard that the glass walls shook she screamed, 'I'll see you in court, you scheming cocksuckers!' It was a brave statement; but it was a false one. Bridget knew in her heart of hearts that she'd slipped up and that even the best lawyer wouldn't be able to protect her from her inevitable fate.

As she stormed out she almost knocked over Richard Stimp – a Cambridge contemporary and the second in command in the Geldlust compliance department. Richard was a short, weaselly jobsworth whose father just happened to be MD of Geldlust's UK operations. He had been an object of derision for Bridget's Cambridge clique who knew him as 'the gimp' – a bitter, angry little Hitler who had hated Bridget's 'cool friends' ever since freshers' week. Throughout Cambridge his laughable attempts to be trendy were the subject of ridicule and his seething jealousy was palpable. These failings were not crimes in themselves. However, he had spent much of his first student year belittling any poor fool who found themselves lower down the food chain than him; four-eyed natural scientists from Cheshire, spotty, autistic pure maths virgins and greasy-haired salad-dodgers from up north had all been the recipients of the tongue-lashings his insecurity demanded. Bridget's gang justified their cruel treatment of him by deeming it to be merely a taste of his own medicine, though it never seemed to have the desired deterrent effect – he was still making freshers' lives hell even in his final year. Richard had clearly only got his position at Geldlust because of his family ties and even here, much to his horror, he remained the object of regular mockery from some of his old tormentors. He was, as

Bridget had once gleefully told him, 'a fucking cost base and not a revenue generator' – surely the worst insult one banker can throw at another.

'I suppose this has something to do with you, needle-prick?' snarled Bridget when she realised who she'd just bumped into.

'No, Bridget . . . I swear I only just found out an hour ago. I promise you I knew nothing about this.' Richard looked genuinely upset. His ratty little eyes seemed almost close to tears.

'Yeah, pull the other one mate, it's got *fucking* bells on! You've always hated us and now at last you've got your revenge. Well, well done, you *fucking* reject!' It was as if nothing had changed since the first time they'd encountered each other at a party in the cellars of King's College, Cambridge. Richard had never seen anything like the goddess who had danced so seductively to the banging house music that Monday night. He had stood transfixed by the vision in front of him, his joy at seeing something so terrifyingly beautiful tempered by the horrifying knowledge that he would almost certainly never get to make love to such a creature. Nevertheless he had gathered the courage to approach her once her foot-stomping revelry had ended. Bridget was sashaying her way towards the bar and Richard had positioned himself so that he could stop her to ask if she wanted a drink when suddenly Rachel appeared and gave her a heartfelt hug. The two girls had walked off arm in arm, giggling, and he had been left hanging. Something in his heart told him that that was how it would always be. When their paths crossed occasionally at Geldlust he would experience that exact same feeling of impotent pointlessness. What made everything worse was that Richard knew that Bridget hadn't even noticed him on that soul-destroying night down in King's College's cellars. That dreadful realisation had merely ensured that the usual recipients of his ire had been punished especially cruelly in the weeks that followed.

'Listen . . . I may not like Steve and Colum and . . . and those boys, but . . . but I've always really liked you . . . I really do like you. Look, I . . . I would do anything to stop this. I was coming over now to try to change their minds.' Richard was barely able to get his words out. He had hardly dared exchange a word with Bridget since she'd joined the bank and this was not how he had hoped their first proper conversation would go.

'If you think I buy that crock of shit you must be mental. Why don't you grow some balls and admit it?'

Richard began to stutter some kind of garbled response but it was too late. Bridget was already halfway down the corridor to the trading floor.

When I heard Bridget's news, which she told me relatively calmly by the water cooler, I couldn't believe it. I had half a mind to march into Chris's office and tender my resignation immediately . . . but then I realised that bonuses were just about to be dished out and that this was no time for heroics.

I completely agreed with Bridget's theory about why they'd done what they'd done and insisted that we go back to the pub to discuss a counter-strategy.

After I'd said my impassioned piece, Bridget looked at me with a deep sadness in her eyes. She placed her hands on my neck and kissed both my cheeks. I could tell she was holding back the tears. After a deep intake of breath she told me that she needed to have some time on her own and that she'd call me over the weekend.

'Don't worry about me, Steve – you know I'll be all right. I'm always all right,' she whispered before striding off towards the lifts.

That was the last thing she ever said to me.

Three

Geldlust Investment Bank, trading floor
Monday, 15 November, 10.25 a.m.

THE MORNING HAD BEEN AN unremitting disaster, even by Monday's extremely low standards. My debauched weekend had involved some serious over-indulgence in rocket fuel MDMA at an all-night techno rave in King's Cross and a post-party scratch and sniff session of truly biblical proportions back at some trendy loser's minimalist warehouse apartment. Despite managing a few hours of sweaty kip on Sunday night I felt this morning as if Tommy Dorsey's Big Band had each taken 500 mics of LSD and set up shop inside my throbbing cranium. Six Nurofen, a double-drop of Berocca and a greasy bacon butty had so far not had the desired recuperative effect. I could barely focus on the three screens in front of me and felt horribly jittery and paranoid. A film of vinegary sweat across my face and my bloodshot, still dilated eyes would convince any objective witness that I was almost certainly a half-dead junkie in the grip of a particularly painful cold turkey and not a high-flying stockbroker at a City bank. An ironic round of applause from the traders as I'd stumbled in – a pale, dishevelled shell of the man I'd been just three days previously – hadn't improved matters. Some important news over the weekend about the ongoing clean-up of BP's oil disaster and some political trouble in Iran that had potential implications for the oil price were adding to my trembling discomfort. The news was important and I had a job to do. I simply had no choice but to call my clients and offer some insightful pearls of wisdom, but I couldn't think straight. My usual unstoppable bullshit sounded false and unconvincing. I was sure that several of them quickly saw through my stuttering gibberish and decided once again to talk to the automatons at Goldmans instead.

I was also worried about Bridget. Her mobile had been switched off since Friday and she hadn't bothered to return any of my increasingly desperate calls. She also hadn't turned up this morning – though that could have been simply because she had been fired with immediate effect. I just didn't know what was happening, as she'd been completely incommunicado, and so my fevered imagination was running wild. Bridget's unwillingness to answer her calls was also a damn shame because on Sunday afternoon, as I'd lain sweat-soaked and paranoid on my leather sofa watching some bollocks 1950s Roman epic on the TV, I'd devised a kind of rescue plan. In late 2007 I'd stumbled upon some senior

Geldlust's staff's involvement in money laundering. My accidental knowledge had forced me to go on the run for almost two years, but it had also given me the leverage to get my old job back once I'd split up with my girlfriend and returned to Blighty penniless. Whilst those directly involved had either disappeared or died I thought that maybe I could use my knowledge to force Geldlust to retain Bridget's services. I'd promised them that the matter would never be mentioned and I'd promised myself that the horrific events of three years ago, like so many banks' recent skulduggery, would be consigned to the dustbin of history. But extreme problems require extreme solutions and I'd resolved to break my commitment to save Bridget's career.

Bridget, unlike me, loved her job, which was something I never understood. She enjoyed manipulating dumbass clients into giving her business by fluttering her baby blues, and the routine that work provided seemed to keep her demons at bay. Her financial success over the last few years had also helped bolster her fragile self-image and enabled her to sit loud and proud at tiresome dinner parties when surrounded by clucking mothers banging on about their gruesome rug rats. Her job really did mean something to her. I knew she'd be lost without it and that without the restrictions provided by a serious career her drug habit would almost certainly spiral out of control. Fergus would have understood that too, and it was the main reason he'd be mad as hell at Geldlust. It was so clear that Geldlust's management had targeted her because she was at a 'dangerous age'. Her minor transgressions would not have been uncovered but for a concerted effort to remove her from the payroll, and if it hadn't been front-running the heartless pricks would have pinned something else on her.

After yet another faltering conversation with a particularly aggressive hedge fund client whom I was failing dismally to get onside I went downstairs to buy a coffee at the in-house Starbucks. It would be my fourth that morning yet I still felt like one of the walking dead – though with noticeably less direction and focus. As I approached the queue I recognised the cheap suit and bad haircut of Richard Stimp just in front of me. Bridget had informed me on Friday that she suspected he was involved in her dismissal, and our occasional mockery of him at Cambridge definitely made him a likely candidate. I stopped dead in my tracks. I'd wanted to confront him at some point but not whilst I was feeling like this. I steadied myself and, after a brief internal deliberation, decided that this chance encounter could be of use to Bridget – provided I could think more coherently than I had over the previous forty-eight hours.

'Hello, Richard – I suppose you're pleased with yourself?' I said, spitting out the words with as much venom as I could muster.

'Oh, hi, Steve. So, I suppose you've heard about what's happened to Bridget?' said Richard, his voice like a wet fart in a beer can. He looked wan but his tired, ratty little face betrayed no emotion. I didn't hate him; I just felt a mild contempt for the constant scheming he'd got up to both at

Cambridge and at Geldlust. At the former, his desperate insecurity had led him to play his peers off against each other whilst spreading malicious rumours about those who displeased him. These attractive life skills had proved invaluable in banking and he had used his position in Compliance to threaten and cajole those around him. In truth, I somewhat regretted the piss-taking we'd subjected him to at university. It wasn't all that much more extreme than the stuff everyone else had received but he was so obviously unable to take it; it had clearly warped his vulnerable personality. After joining Geldlust I'd wanted to apologise to him, but whenever I'd been bladdered enough to consider broaching the subject at some post-work knees-up he'd always given me such a wide berth that I'd never got round to it.

'Don't act the innocent, you little shit,' I hissed. 'We all know that this was probably your doing – some nasty payback for the way we treated you at Cambridge.' I was keeping my voice to a low whisper so that the others in the queue weren't privy to our conversation. His rapid-fire retort was somewhat more potent that I'd anticipated. I realised immediately that I should have chosen my battleground more wisely.

'Firstly, I couldn't care less what you and your loser friends think. Secondly, it had nothing to do with me. Thirdly, those days are long gone and I feel no need for revenge and fourthly, do you honestly think it would be Bridget I'd target out of all you dicks if I wanted to get back at your little group? Grow up, Steve!'

I stood there stunned at the comprehensive dressing-down I'd just received. Before I could think of a suitably biting response Richard had turned his back, bought his coffee and scuttled off – no doubt to trawl through my recent emails hoping to find something incriminating. If he tried that he'd be sorely disappointed; I'd been so scrupulously careful since my return to Geldlust that he'd find nothing. Any front-running or insider trading I'd undertaken with clients had always been done face to face in the corner of some nameless bar. I'd thought Bridget had been smart enough to know the rules of the game; obviously I had been wrong.

I returned to my desk feeling distinctly uneasy. I called Bridget's mobile and her home phone number for the third time that morning and, once again, was greeted by her cheery answerphone message. I sat there, ignoring the usual mid-morning trading floor banter, staring into the middle distance pondering what to do. I couldn't rid myself of this terrible anxiety that was gnawing away at my insides. I felt sure that it wasn't just the drugs still racing around my system that were making me feel so nervous.

Three minutes later my phone rang. Assuming it was some client requiring sensible advice I had half a mind to ignore it, but after a few rings and some quizzical looks from my neighbouring colleagues I steadied myself and picked up the receiver. It wasn't a client; it was Rachel.

'Hi, Steve. How are you?'

I hadn't spoken to Rachel for a couple of weeks. Just like

Bridget, Rachel had lost her job as a research analyst in the transport sector at Geldlust almost exactly two years before during the annual pre-bonus lay-offs. She had been absolutely gutted at the time and had formulated various conspiracy theories about why she'd been fired. At one point she was convinced that Richard had been behind it and for another, especially paranoid moment had even concluded that her supposed best friend Bridget had had something to do with it, which was of course total nonsense. The fact was that she was a married woman in her mid-thirties who had already taken off two lots of maternity leave and was likely to do so again. The profit-hungry tossers in Geldlust's management were understandably upset by this unreasonable urge to start a family and decided to mete out a suitable punishment. After she'd been shown the door and finally decided not to take Geldlust to court she spent several frustrating months failing to find a position at another investment bank. It was late 2008, the peak of the financial crisis, and banking jobs were as rare as hen's teeth. Eventually, she'd swallowed her pride and secured a role at the City regulator, the FSA. Here she was set the task of investigating accusations of insider trading . . . which, luckily for her, was something she happened to know a lot about having engaged in some hands-on research many times before. Despite the brave face she put on we all knew that she missed the buzz and excitement of stockbroking and detested her new job. Whenever we met for a drink she'd ask nostalgically about certain notorious characters on the trading floor and refuse to talk about the mundanity of her new responsibilities. Her fun side still peeped over the parapet when we were together but her new role had made her more jaded . . . it was either that or the fact that she was sharing her life with a beige man in a beige suburb with two beige kids.

'Not too hot, actually . . . after battering it all night on Saturday I feel like I've contracted a bad case of wine flu,' I joked. 'I'm getting way too old for this shit!'

'Well, listen . . . are you sitting down?' Her tone was worryingly subdued. I steadied myself for some bad news.

'A colleague of mine has a friend who works as a secretary at Merrills. Anyway, this girl lives at her boyfriend's in the Barbican and apparently as she was walking to work this morning she passed a police cordon and one of those forensic tents in the middle of the road. She asked the policemen what was going on and they told her that some-one had committed suicide by jumping from the one of the towers . . . a woman. Look, I don't know who it is and it's probably nothing but . . . well, you know where Bridget lives and I heard about what happened on Friday . . .' Rachel's voice trailed off. My stomach immediately turned to water.

'What . . . what? I'll go over there . . . but . . . but . . . who told you she'd been sacked?' My voice had risen an octave or two out of sheer panic. I was already getting some strange looks from the salesmen who sat around me.

'Actually she told me herself . . . that's the thing. She left me a few voicemails on Saturday morning saying how she'd lost her job and how depressed she was about everything. The awful thing is . . . I never got back to her. On Saturday I was busy with the kids and on Sunday I had a major argument with Darren . . . I only tried to call her today after I'd heard about this suicide.' I could sense a touch of guilt in Rachel's tone. Her relationship with Bridget had always been a little odd. They met in freshers' week and were joined at the hip by the end of the first term but there was always a strange dynamic between the two; Rachel envied Bridget's effortless beauty whilst Bridget was often unsympathetic about Rachel's seeming inability to attract decent men. Still, they'd generally been there for each other through thick and thin – though evidently not this time.

'Don't beat yourself up. I'm sure she's fine . . . I'm going over to her flat right now . . . we'll probably all be laughing about this come midday,' I stuttered. I was desperately trying to sound cheerful but couldn't overcome the awful feeling that had embedded itself in the acidic pit of my knotted stomach. My heart was pounding and the noxious damp patches under my arms were expanding by the second. That something might have happened to my Bridge was too terrible to contemplate, especially in the state I was in.

I swiftly terminated the conversation with Rachel by telling her I'd call her as soon as I had any news. I then snatched my jacket from the back of my chair and, without saying a word to my fellow salesmen, hurried off towards the lifts.

Four

The Barbican
Monday, 15 November, 11.35 a.m.

THE TAXI TOOK SEVEN MINUTES to reach the Barbican. When I saw the yellow and black tape blocking the road directly in front of Bridget's flat I took a few deep gulps of air. I could feel myself beginning to shake uncontrollably.

'Sorry, mate, I can't go no further. Looks like there's been a shooting or sumfink . . .' The taxi driver's nasal tones snapped me out of my daze. I handed him a tenner and didn't bother waiting for the change. I steadied myself, got out and walked towards the youthful policeman standing guard.

'Hi. My girlfriend lives in this building . . . erm, could you tell me . . . what's going on?' I was surprised that I'd actually managed to get the words out.

'I'm afraid a woman has fallen to her death.' My already racing heart beat went up a notch.

'Look, could you tell me her name? My girlfriend lives up there . . . Please!' My hands were outstretched in front of me, begging. I'm not quite sure why I was referring to Bridget as my girlfriend – it just slipped out. Maybe it was panic, maybe I'd thought he'd be more likely to disclose the information I required . . . or maybe it was just wishful thinking. Whatever the reason, I'd live to regret that particular decision.

'I'm very sorry, but we can't divulge that information. We need to inform her family first. However, I can tell you that the woman in question fell from that window there.' He pointed up at a tenth-floor window. Bridget lived on the tenth floor but I couldn't tell if it was her flat or one of the ones next to hers. I held back the tears and pleaded with God for it not to be her window.

'Oh, Christ! Fuck! Look . . . look . . . is it someone called Bridget Von Blixen? She's my girlfriend . . . *I have to know!*' The sheer panic in my voice startled the policeman. He looked at me with concern. He was clearly mulling over whether to tell me something . . . or, worse, *how* to tell me something.

'Just wait there a minute,' he said after a long pause. He walked away a few paces and spoke quietly into the radio attached to his shoulder. I craned my head, desperate to hear what he was saying. I could just make out his first words.

'Sarge . . . we've got someone here who claims to be the boyfriend . . .'

I didn't hear the rest of what he said. I simply dropped to my knees, held my head in my hands and started sobbing uncontrollably. I thought I was going to be sick. I gagged several times. I tried to take some breaths but found that my throat had squeezed shut, and frantically gulped for air. The immediate feeling of loss was unbearable. The tears streamed down my face. I couldn't believe this was happening.

After a few minutes I felt a hand on my shoulder. I stood up unsteadily and saw the concerned face of the young policeman. He knew that I knew and was clearly unsure how to handle the situation. After a few moments he simply said: 'I'm sorry.'

By this stage I'd just about got my whimpering under control. I was still sobbing like a child but I was breathing more steadily. I couldn't believe that Bridge was gone – for ever. Suddenly out of nowhere I heard someone scream 'NO' as loudly as they could . . . it was a few seconds before I realised it was me.

The young policeman made me sit down and wait for his sergeant who he told me was busy investigating Bridget's flat. I sat on the kerb staring at the ground, slowly beginning to get my laboured breathing under control. After about five minutes I heard footsteps approach me and a deep, kindly voice spoke.

'Hello. Would you like a cup of tea? There's a café just

round the corner.' I looked up. The man I assumed to be the sergeant was around forty with a long nose, a thick moustache and bright, intelligent eyes.

I carefully pulled myself up and silently followed him to a greasy spoon called Mr Patel's. He left me at a Formica table by the window staring into space whilst he went to the counter, returning with two chipped mugs overflowing with builder's tea. He placed one in front of me and lowered himself into his chair, and for some time we just sat there in total silence, taking the odd sip from our mugs. I felt an overpowering numbness envelop me. I wanted to cry, but there were no tears left. We could have been there a minute, or maybe an hour, before the sergeant spoke. His voice was low and comforting.

'I'm Sergeant David Miller and I'm going to be in charge of investigating this . . . situation.' He was clearly unsure about what word to use – I supposed that it wasn't a crime but still a police matter.

'First of all let me say how sorry I am. A death like this is always tragic, and she was a beautiful young woman who seemed to have a lot to live for.' I listened to his clichéd platitudes and said nothing, merely nodding my agreement.

After a suitably long pause he removed a little black notebook from his inside jacket pocket and started asking me the usual questions. After finding out my name, address, mobile number and current employer he immediately cut to the chase and asked me the question I was beginning to realise was inevitable.

'So tell me, how long have you been Bridget's boyfriend?'

My heart sank into my stomach as I remembered that I'd just told these coppers a blatant lie. Some sick paranoid part of me queried again whether my mendacity had been brought on by wishful thinking. Whatever my motivation, I felt a sudden wave of uneasiness. To contradict myself now would make me look foolish and probably end in the swift termination of our conversation and I desperately needed to know what had happened; on the other hand, to keep up the pretence could mean that I'd be exposed at a later date and for all I knew it might even be classified as perjury. After a brief pause I chose to continue with my lie.

'Well . . . we've been seeing each other for . . . for . . . almost a year . . . but we've been great mates since university – almost twenty years – and we work . . . we . . . we worked together in the City,' I stammered.

'OK,' he said, an elongated second syllable and slight inflexion suggesting he wasn't entirely convinced by my answer. I've always struggled when lying to coppers, as my numerous run-ins with them over the years have proved pretty conclusively, and this day was no exception. Nevertheless, he continued: 'And when did you last see her?'

'Well, at around four p.m. on Friday at work.' I was beginning to see that my whole boyfriend story might sound a bit implausible as I only lived fifteen minutes' walk away from her and yet we'd spent the whole weekend apart. I started trying to think up some possible explanation for this suspiciously long separation. I thought that maybe I should claim we'd had an argument but quickly realised that that could put me in a compromising situation. My heart began pounding and I felt my armpits dampen. I was seriously regretting my impulsive lie but it was too late to go back now.

'You see, I wanted to go out partying this weekend and she wanted to stay in and take it easy . . .' I was struggling badly here, hardly convincing myself let alone this nosy cop. I was close to confessing that I was full of shit when Sergeant Miller asked another question.

'And tell me . . . did she display any signs of being depressed or even . . . suicidal recently?' His eyes narrowed as he sought out the truth.

'No, no, not at all . . . well, erm, I suppose she'd got some pretty bad news on Friday. You see . . . she lost her job and she lost it in such a way that she probably couldn't ever work again in finance. She seemed sad but . . . but she's not the type to do this kind of thing. She loved life . . .' My voice tailed off as I heard myself speak of her in the past tense. I felt like crying again but stopped myself. I also suddenly realised that, to the sergeant, my choosing to party rather than comfort her over the weekend after she'd just been fired made me look like a heartless prick. Thinking about all these complications was making me piss sweat but it was also helping to take my mind off the true horror of the situation. While I was worrying about getting my story straight I wasn't thinking about the gaping hole that had just appeared in my life.

The sergeant was speaking again. 'Yes, well, there is another factor that I feel able to discuss with you since you *are* her boyfriend...' This sounded horribly ominous. 'Did Bridget ever take drugs? And please do not feel the need to protect her for her family's sake or anything like that... we are *very* discreet in these matters.' Christ, this was like the fucking Spanish Inquisition. Again, I tried to get my mashed potato brain to think as fast as it could about the potential implications of my words... not just for her but for me as her 'boyfriend'. As I pondered a suitable response I suddenly remembered I had a wrap containing half a gram of toot in my wallet left over from my grotty weekend. I gulped and looked up, hoping the sergeant couldn't read my thoughts. His unblinking eyes seemed to bore straight into me. My paranoia had now taken full control.

'Yeah, well... erm... I mean she's a... she's known to... erm... perhaps very occasionally indulge... you know, she's, she was, a... a beautiful woman who liked to have fun... I obviously disapproved but, hey, girls will be girls.' The false cheeriness of my last words suddenly seemed horribly unfeeling. My worries about being implicated in something were making me forget why I was here: a girl I adored was dead. I would never see her again; I would never talk to her again... I broke down in tears.

'I know this must be hard for you,' Sergeant Miller said, leaning across the table and patting my shoulder. After a minute or so I managed to get my sobs under control.

'Why did you ask me about drugs?'

'Well, and I want you to keep this strictly between you and me, there was obvious evidence of extensive drug use in her living room. Lots of traces of white powder on the table, what looks like a crack pipe that's had recent use, wraps of granulated material that we suspect is MDMA or ketamine . . . the full works. I'm afraid I don't think she responded to the news of her dismissal by "taking it easy" . . . far from it, in fact.'

Fuck! So she'd left me on Friday afternoon, immediately scored a truckload of pharmaceuticals, gone home and battered it. Oh, shit . . . that's just the way she would have dealt with the bad news and she was already pretty wired when she left me. She'd got straight back into her old habits as if she'd never left them. She'd probably spent the whole weekend glued to the mirror and the razor blade, pausing only to take the odd lick from the crack pipe. Things were beginning to fit into place. But I just couldn't believe that she would have sat there by herself getting high. That just wasn't her style. She thought people who did that were two-bit losers and she always craved someone to talk at when she was buzzing. And she couldn't have simply sat there getting frazzled with her actual boyfriend because Fergus had become increasingly anti-drugs. He knew she used to be a proper coke-head and wouldn't allow any snorting whilst he was around. He was pretty militant about it and I'd witnessed some quite harrowing arguments when he'd correctly suspected her of pepping herself up during one of our social gatherings. In fact, since they'd got together she had generally hidden from him the minor drug usage that she still engaged in. It struck me that it was highly likely she'd been caning it with someone else. I thought for a few seconds and then asked another question.

'Was anyone with her . . . you know . . . at the end? Was anyone in the room with her?' I watched Sergeant Miller's narrow, angular face very carefully for clues but it betrayed nothing. The man's poker face was undoubtedly more practised than my own.

'Actually, we don't know at the moment. We're talking to everyone who might have seen something and we'll be putting up signs on the street hoping that some local resident can help us out. A lot of people were on their way to work this morning and one of them must have seen something.' He paused for a minute and then looked up at me. 'We're also dusting the room for prints and DNA. It's a real mess up there but there's a hell of a lot of glasses and stuff covered in the remnants of what looks like quite a party. If . . .' He paused. I could tell he was about to ask me for some kind of favour. 'Look, if you could tell me who her close friends were then we could take all their prints and cross-check them with those in the room. That way we'd be able to see if there were any strangers' prints there. We'd promise not to keep them on record . . . they'd be doing us, and Bridget, a big favour. Do you think you could do that?'

As far as I knew Bridget didn't hang out with anyone apart from the five of us from university. She hadn't made any good friends at work – at least not the sort to cane drugs with back at her flat. I thought for a few seconds. I didn't want to get any of our mutual pals in trouble but I also wanted to help the police find out if there was anything more to Bridget's death than a drugged-up suicide. Even if she had been on elephantine quantities of Class A I still couldn't believe that she'd have taken her own life. There just had to be more to it.

'OK, I'll give you their names and their mobile numbers. There's only really six of us in the crew. We're all old friends from Cambridge. But if I do this I want you to give me your number and keep me informed about what's going on.'

'Well, I'm not going to give out any sensitive information that could impact on the investigation, but I can promise to tell you anything we find out if there's a mutual benefit in doing so. So, tell me the names of the people in your "crew" . . . oh, and by the way, we'll be needing your prints too, of course.'

After giving Miller all the information he required I stood up and we shook hands. We had agreed that I'd come to the station on Wednesday afternoon to give my prints and a DNA swab of my gums. I was just about to leave the café when, in classic Detective Columbo fashion, Miller said: 'Oh, just one more thing . . .'

My heart sank as I envisaged him pointing out some obvious contradiction in my story. As soon as I heard those words I was convinced that my whole boyfriend act was about to be exposed as a tissue of lies and that I would have to 'accompany him to the station' for obstructing justice or some such shit. I half expected to be cuffed and anally probed there and then.

'Yeah, what?' I said, perhaps a little too aggressively.

'Bridget's cat. I don't suppose you'd look after it, or find it a new owner?'

I almost laughed out loud in relief. Of course: Mr Tibbs, Bridget's grey Burmese cat, was now an orphan. I'd never particularly liked the aggressive little fucker and he had a nasty habit of digging his claws into my gonads, but I felt obliged to do the decent thing.

'No probs. I'll be happy to take him. It's the least I can do.'

Miller radioed one of his colleagues in Bridget's flat, who appeared five minutes later holding a startled-looking Mr Tibbs. I gingerly took him in my arms, walked to the main road and began looking for a taxi to take us home. There was no way in hell I was going back to work after what I'd just heard. The way I was feeling, I'd probably take the whole decade off.

Once Mr Tibbs and I were settled into my flat on Old Street I steadied myself for what I knew would be one of the most agonizing experiences of my entire life. I sat in the near dark of my living room staring at my BlackBerry for what seemed like hours. The curtains were closed and the only noises were those of cars in the distance. I couldn't bring myself to make the call but I knew I had to. I had to be strong but I was running on empty and close to breaking down myself. Eventually I gathered up all the depleted resources I had left and rang him. He answered after two rings.

'Hello?'

'Hi, Fergus, it's . . . it's Steve.' My voice was trembling with emotion. I was desperately holding back the tears.

'Hi, mate. What's up? You sound upset.' Fergus's deep voice with its Scottish lilt was as strong and firm as it always was. His relaxed demeanour made what I had to say all the more horrifying.

'Listen, are you sitting down? I've got something terrible to tell you. I don't think there's a right way of doing this . . . so I'm just going to say it.' I took a deep breath.

'OK.' He still sounded calm and strong, but you never knew how Fergus felt about anything. I'd always sensed that he never really let me know what was going on in his head ever since we'd first met at school.

'OK . . . OK . . .' I took another deep breath. 'Bridget's dead. They found her body on the road outside her flat this morning. They think it was suicide.'

For what seemed like an eternity there was almost no sound at all. I could just hear Fergus's deep breathing. Then suddenly from nowhere I heard an awful cry of anguished pain. The terrible sound continued for a few seconds. I tried and failed to get my own crying under control. Then Fergus took a long, deep breath and between howls tried to say something. I couldn't grasp what it was because he was sobbing too violently to get it out. After a few minutes he began to get some control over his crying and I finally understood what he'd been saying.

'We'd just got engaged. We'd just got engaged.'

Five

The William IV pub, Harrow Road
Saturday, 20 November, 1.15 p.m.

THE FUNERAL HAD, WITHOUT DOUBT, been the most depressing two hours of my entire life and that was following five of the most dismal days I'd so far experienced on this sorry planet. I'd had no choice but to take the whole week off – a decision that was helped by a minor bout of Colombian flu brought on by the previous weekend's excesses. But there was another reason, apart from the unbearable sadness caused by Bridget's death, that had made going into work impossible: I also felt morally repulsed by Geldlust. We'd always known that under-performers got fired in December before bonuses were dished out, but as long as no one close to us fell victim to this brutal treatment we didn't really care about it. Indeed, we fortunate winners who survived December's unlucky list would actually benefit from the reduced number of noses in the bonus trough. Hence the heartfelt sorrow we expressed as we shook the hands of those poor muppets who'd fallen at the last hurdle was always tinged with an element of joy as we calculated the minor percentage increase to our own bonus that each dismissal represented. Bridget's sacking was all the more horrifying because she had actually exceeded her commission targets. If she really had committed suicide then there was no doubt that Geldlust had blood on their hands. Frankly, I couldn't bear the idea of ever going back to work and striving to make profits for my best friend's murderers.

During the week we'd all been on the phone to each other as we tried our best to support one another and come to terms with our shared tragedy. I told them all to expect a call from the police asking them to come in to give their fingerprints and a DNA swab. John and Colum kicked up a surprisingly angry fuss but I told them that the police had promised that the samples would be destroyed as soon as the investigation was concluded. They started banging on about its being an infringement of their civil rights but eventually they saw the sense of playing ball with the police. I had been slightly embarrassed as each asked me in turn why on earth I had pretended to be Bridget's boyfriend, but I explained that the cops would almost certainly have told me nothing had I said that I was merely a friend and that I was desperate to find out the truth on that awful Monday morning. Even Fergus seemed satisfied with this explanation though it was difficult to tell as he merely grunted down the line. He did manage to get across to me that Bridget had left a message on his mobile on Friday afternoon claiming that she was going to stay at her mother's country cottage for the weekend and that they'd hook up on Monday. That explained why he hadn't seen her on Saturday or Sunday.

Several of us met up to help each other get over our loss; I know that John and Rachel shared a near silent dinner together and that Colum and Rachel had a sombre lunch-time coffee at the Royal Exchange. Rachel and I also met for a drink, and after our initial tears we reminisced about Bridget and the life she'd led. Over a few gin and Slimline tonics, Rachel reminded me of one particularly debauched punting trip down the Cam to Grantchester Meadows that all six of us had enjoyed. It had been a blazing hot day in June a few days after the end of our second year exams. We had all consumed some unexpectedly poky acid and were tripping like demented bullfrogs before we'd even negotiated our way out of Cambridge. We also had enough puff and scrumpy to ensure that we'd be seriously befuddled long before we made it to the Green Man in Grantchester. A huge Nigerian briefcase that we'd positioned perilously close to the edge at one end of the punt blared out the latest cheesy house music and vast hordes of tourists stood and stared at the half-naked weirdos frolicking around in the afternoon sun. Fergus, like Neal Cassady for the Merry Pranksters, always took it upon himself to drive, or in this case punt, the group whenever we were high. He had an uncanny ability to remain focused no matter how many chemicals he'd ingested. He stood at the punt's rear like a

Colossus pushing us towards our goal whilst we smoked, drank and laughed until we could laugh no more.

Bridget had been on brilliant form that day. We had split up by then but I was still madly in love with her. She sat at the front of the punt facing forward like a perfectly sculpted figurehead for a ship of fools going nowhere slowly. When we reached the clipped lawn of the Newnham Riverbank Club I had told the group that this was where Virginia Woolf and Rupert Brooke had swum naked almost a century before. On hearing this, Bridget immediately removed her loose summer dress and underwear and jumped naked into the water – much to the surprise of the schoolboys who were sitting on the lawn. She goaded us to follow her but only Colum was brave enough to jump in naked – which proved even more of a shock to the wide-eyed schoolboys. Rachel had entered the water tentatively and almost succeeded in capsizing the punt as she eased herself in. Of course, she had kept her M&S pants and T-shirt on because, as always, she felt fat and frumpy next to Bridget. Those minutes floating around and splashing each other were some of the happiest of my life. I can still recall Bridget's slender, pale body gliding through the silky water and her hearty laugh filling the air. Everything seemed perfect, though an ache deep within me, which had been there since Bridget and I had finished, reminded me even on that glorious afternoon that all was not as I'd like it to be . . . and maybe never would be again.

When we finally made it to the Green Man we were

faced with a terrible quandary: who should enter its dark confines in order to buy the golden lagers that lay within? Colum and I were definitely way too confused to even contemplate such an expedition. Rachel was shaking her head even before the conversation turned to her. Bridget had no qualms about going in but I wouldn't let her because she'd somehow managed to get her dress soaking wet and it had gone practically see-through. John was staring intently at a patch of grass and mumbling something about Paisley patterns so he didn't seem like the prime candidate for this particular mission. Accordingly, it was Fergus. I watched with envy as he nonchalantly bought six lagers and brought them to us in the beer garden on a tray with neither the giggling nor the guaranteed mishap that would have accompanied me. There was certainly a look of approval from Bridget after that flawless performance. I couldn't help feeling horribly jealous and would later wonder whether that was when she first fell in love with him. Was that when the seeds of their relationship were sown? Rachel and I laughed and cried as we recalled details of that momentous day. She held my hand across the table and tears rolled down her cheeks at each new addition to the story. Other customers at the café stared at us but we didn't care; we just missed our friend.

The day after my depressing drink with Rachel, I hooked up with John for a coffee. He had been with the rest of us on that notorious punting extravaganza, but even back then his approach to drug-taking had been different from ours.

Whereas we used drugs to enhance fun situations, to him they had always been the goal in themselves. He had looked as though he loved being on that punt but I suspect he would have been just as content locked in a dark cupboard on his own with the same mix of pharmaceuticals racing around his system. Whilst John wanted to be one of the gang, he was also enviably self-contained.

Unfortunately, my chat with him didn't go smoothly. After some more nostalgic reminiscing I decided to broach the subject of his 'stalking' Bridget. As soon as I mentioned it he became prickly and defensive. I tried to downplay the whole episode but he just sat there with his arms crossed glaring at me. I started getting angry at his teenage stone-walling and was about to get up and go when suddenly he broke the silence. He explained through gritted teeth that he had simply seen Bridget by chance in the street and, 'for a laugh', decided to follow her. He insisted that it was not 'stalking', as I had put it, but just a curious friend following another merely to find out what they got up to when they were alone. When I told him that I knew about his declaration of love his face darkened. Eventually, he admitted that he'd always held a candle for Bridget but he maintained that he'd had 'a bit of Boutros' before he'd seen her that day and that his mouth had been running away with him. I tried to broach the subject of Bridget's death but that just brought back the silent treatment. I'd spent enough time with John to recognise that he wasn't telling me everything he knew about Bridget's demise. He never was any good at lying but I let it go, and after I'd used all my skills of diplomacy to placate him we parted company friends.

In the immediate aftermath of Bridget's death no one could persuade Fergus to come out for a face-to-face chat. I tried desperately to convince him to meet me but he was immovable. He hadn't turned up for work at the *Guardian* and had spent the entire week sitting alone in the depths of despair. On Wednesday I paid a visit to his flat off Brick Lane but he wasn't in; or at least he refused to answer his bell. On Thursday I called Bridget's mum to express my deepest condolences. She was completely inconsolable. Bridget had been her only child and there was a deep bond between them brought about by Bridget's father's suddenly running off with a woman half his age twenty years before. The string of unsuitable, and occasionally violent, lovers Diane Von Blixen had subsequently fallen into the arms of had no doubt contributed to Bridget's fragile emotional state. Diane had informed me that the coroner had already released the body and the funeral would take place in two days' time.

I met Rachel at Colum's palatial penthouse flat off Hoxton Square at 9.30 a.m. on the Saturday and the three of us shared a minicab to Kensal Green cemetery. We hardly exchanged a word for the whole journey. Even Colum, a man prone to making boorish, inappropriate remarks whenever possible, just stared mournfully out of the taxi window. This was no time for small talk and there was nothing we could say about Bridget's death that would make any of us feel better. It was a grey, blustery morning and I felt bitterly cold despite my woollen suit and thick overcoat. We filed into the chapel and, on seeing John and Fergus sitting together, settled ourselves into three free seats behind them. I placed a hand on Fergus's shoulder but he didn't turn round – he just continued staring straight ahead. John and I exchanged quiet greetings and then I sat back.

The chapel was about half full; around seventy dark-suited people sat in near total silence. I looked around for faces I recognised and saw Bridget's mother at the front. A tall, dapper man of about sixty-five who I suspected was Bridget's father sat about ten feet to her right. I knew that they hated each other but at least it appeared that he had had the good grace not to bring the woman who had split up Bridget's family and caused her and her mother so much grief. There were also a few representatives from Geldlust – several salespeople and a couple of analysts whom Bridget had befriended. I also saw about five of her best clients and a couple of Geldlust executives. The presence of the MDs irritated me as I couldn't help but see them as the enemy – a bunch of slimy pig fuckers who had indirectly played a role in Bridget's demise. I was pleased to notice that the despicable little prick Richard had not dared show his ugly mug on a day I was beginning to hold him and his hideous Nazi cohorts responsible for.

The service was a humanist one as neither Bridget nor her bohemian mum had any truck with God-bothering.

Diane, dressed in a rather eccentric billowing navy blue dress, gave a painfully emotional, strained address at the beginning of the ceremony that brought tears to the eyes of our entire group. A cousin of Bridget's whom she had always been close to read out a poem by Somerset Maugham, though she was in such a state that I only caught a few words of it through her sobs. A stolid uncle, who was clearly a fervent bible-basher, made a rather staid speech about 'the Christian way' and the bountiful afterlife that such a path would bestow on those who followed it. Understandably, no one mentioned the fact that Bridget had almost certainly taken it upon herself to shuffle off her mortal coil.

Towards the end of the service Fergus stood up and walked to the podium. He paused for what seemed like an eternity before gathering himself and delivering a heart-breaking portrayal of the amazing person he had loved so dearly. He managed to avoid crying but it was obvious to everyone that at any second he could have broken down. His Scottish burr and deep voice only made his words more moving.

We filed out after about an hour and gathered outside for a cigarette. I saw Diane talking tearfully to Bridget's cousin, and after steadying myself I went over to express my sympathy to them both. We had a brief hug and then I rejoined our group and had another brooding cigarette. I didn't really smoke usually but this was no time for rules. After a few minutes of puffing away I saw Fergus approach Diane and they had what seemed like a terse conversation.

They ended their exchange with a very awkward hug that Diane seemed reluctant to engage in. It was quite clear even from ten yards away that she didn't like Fergus – either that or they had had some disagreement over the past week.

Fergus approached our group with his usual stiff gait. His eyes were bloodshot and had huge dark bags under them. He stood there with drooping shoulders for a few seconds and, after bumming a cigarette from Colum, said in a resigned, weary voice, 'Let's go to the fucking pub.' We walked off without saying a word towards the William IV.

'Yeah, let's punish those pricks! Let's show those filthy wankers who's boss!' slurred Colum, who was blatantly more arseholed than the rest of us. Whilst we had been supping our pints gently, as seemed appropriate for the sombre occasion, he had been downing his with frightening speed and I had even spied him knocking back a few sneaky shots of Sambuca when he was alone at the bar. I also couldn't help but notice that he'd been making regular trips to the gents and wondered whether he was sufficiently ill-mannered to be getting coked-up at a wake. Frankly, I'd put nothing past him. About half an hour before his outburst I'd followed him into the toilets to stop him doing any more nozz-up, but this time he was taking a legitimate horse piss in a urinal and I had followed suit. It was strange, but during those brief moments in the gents together I got the strong impression that he really wanted to tell me something. He kept skirting around the issue of Bridget's death and then returning to it. It was as if he wanted to divulge some significant piece of information but didn't quite have the balls to do it. The familiar Charlie-induced desire to reveal even the most personal of secrets seemed to be battling with an equally strong urge to keep this particular confession under wraps. I didn't press him but his behaviour was making me uneasy.

'*Cunts!* All of them! Let's do 'em all . . . *now!*' he was shouting, banging his chubby fist on the table, his Australian drawl making everything he said sound even more aggressive. Colum had picked up his odd Australian inflexion from a five-year stay in Melbourne during his teens and compounded the error by sporting a bizarre mullet-type haircut that I can only imagine was also some sick throwback to his Antipodean adolescence. When questioned about his unusual hairstyle he would gleefully extol its virtues, claiming it was 'office at the front, party at the back' as if that justified looking like Michael Bolton circa 1995. His bizarre appearance was all the more unusual because he suffered from a mild form of rosacea. This meant that after a few drinks his face would begin to resemble a baboon's scarlet arse . . . and what generally came out of it was as predictably offensive.

At Cambridge he'd had a brief affair with Rachel and that's how he'd become part of our group. His behaviour back then was already generally obnoxious but I suppose we took him, genital warts and all, because he made us laugh as well as cry. He once proudly told us that he'd spent his gap year doing charitable deeds . . . and when questioned further explained that he'd received a large inheritance on his eighteenth birthday and had travelled to places like Bangkok, Amsterdam and Havana giving a lot of his money to young women with AIDS. It took about three months for me to realise that his 'charitable work' involved face-fucking impoverished brasses at brothels across the globe. When I finally asked him if that was what he meant he merely smirked and said with his laconic Australian drawl, 'Look, I gave those poor women the money as a charitable gift; the fact that they misinterpreted my kind gesture and chose to nosh me off is, frankly, irrelevant.' He went on to explain that he fully agreed with Errol Flynn's stated view that 'the best way to get to know a country is through its whorehouses'. It beggared belief that whilst some noble souls had spent their gap year teaching trigonometry to orphans in Nepal, Colum had simply moved from one red light district to another – literally shagging his way around the world. Ever since those halcyon days his basic philosophy was best summed up by his most oft-used expression: 'if it floats, flies or fucks . . . rent it' – a profound belief system he adhered to religiously. The man hadn't lost his moral compass . . . he'd sold it long ago for a quick bunk-up at a Filipino whorehouse.

'Yes, well, thank you for those considered words, Colum,' Fergus muttered, rolling his eyes. 'We always appreciate your wisdom in these matters.' Colum was so wasted that he didn't even recognise Fergus's weary irony.

'That's right, bro, let's do something spectacular,' he

drivelled, patting Fergus vigorously on the back. 'Let's make those snivelling toerags rue the day they were fucking born.'

'And what, may I ask, would you propose we do?' Fergus spat out the words – his growing irritation was blindingly obvious to the rest of us but was still completely lost on Colum who had definitely come loose from his moorings. Colum, unlike Fergus, was certainly no stranger to going 'full retard', but there was a certain desperation in his drinking that compounded my earlier feelings of disquiet. Something was rotten in the borough of Brent.

'Erm . . . I don't know . . . some . . . some fucking thing,' Colum slurred, rubbing his nostrils vigorously.

During the preliminary drinks I had explained in precise detail why Bridget believed she'd been fired. It all made perfect sense and no one amongst us doubted that she had been the victim of a despicable conspiracy, probably involving our old friend Richard Stimp. During the discussion sorrow had, to some extent, been replaced by anger. Fergus, not known for having a long fuse, had been clenching and unclenching his fists for the best part of two hours. He also had a furious look in his eye that I'd only seen a few times before – most notably during a fight with some outback hicks we'd got into a drinking competition with when we were in Australia. Our few weeks together surfing in Queensland were for me the start of my pre-university gap year but for Fergus they were merely a short holiday before he joined the army. We thought we were headed in completely different directions and hence the whole trip had assumed a massive significance for two old school friends who were just about wise enough to know that things might never be the same again. I can't remember exactly how the fight between us and those three lumberjack-shirt-wearing mongoloids started; all I remember is how it ended – with Fergus swinging a barroom stool into the faces of our adversaries. We drove out of that two-horse mining town pretty sharpish after that encounter, unsure as to the extent of the damage we'd caused but pretty damn sure that there was an SUV full of web-toed cousins just round the corner who would come after us with Daddy's rifle given half a chance. We had left bloodied and bruised but laughing like two maniacs. It had been the last week of our holiday together and a seemingly appropriate bonding session for two old mates whose paths seemed like they were about to deviate for good. Little did we know then that the army would not agree with Fergus nor he with it, and that, after a nine-month term of service, he would somehow manage to extricate himself from the military and, even better, end up in Cambridge as a last-minute entrant to Anglia Polytechnic – a red-brick educational facility that wasn't a part of the university, a fact that Colum repeatedly reminded him of.

'Maybe we could do something . . . something smart,' John suddenly piped up. He'd been virtually silent for the last two hours and, since he rarely dared to speak up, his words made an immediate impact. As usual he'd spent his time in the pub picking at his head, tugging out the few remaining hairs on his temples. We all knew he had some weird condition, something I'd once Googled that was called trichotillomania – a compulsive urge to pull out his own hair brought about by severe anxiety. Judging by the Jack Nicholsonesque widow's peak he was developing his nervous habit had gone into overdrive over the past week.

'Like what?' asked Rachel, putting her hand on Colum's knee again. She'd already rested it there several times and she kept looking drunkenly into his eyes whilst he was spouting his meaningless bullshit. She'd also been crying intermittently and banging on about how she 'should have been there for Bridget'. She wasn't a good drunk at the best of times and this session seemed to be resulting in textbook clichéd pissed behaviour – alternating between slurred, tactile 'I love you' type nonsense and mournful self-pity. We had all, apart from Fergus who had noticeably remained stony-faced on hearing her doleful self-criticism, been trying our best to persuade her that she could have done nothing to prevent the tragedy. Unsurprisingly, she seemed to not be listening. Rachel had developed a habit of beating herself up over perceived failings and Bridget's death looked as if it was going to provide her with enough guilt to last her until her own dying day.

'Well, maybe together we could do some kind of . . . "bank job"?'

'Oh yeah?' sneered Colum. Suddenly, and without warning, he turned round to face him. 'And talking of jobs, John, do you remember your first *blow* job?'

We were all taken aback by Colum's sudden lowering of

the tone. I saw Fergus stare daggers at him and Rachel's mouth dropped in disbelief at what she'd heard. After an embarrassingly long silence, a deeply suspicious John tentatively replied, 'Erm, yes, as a matter of fact I do.'

'Oh yeah? Great! And tell me, did he come?' Colum had barely got the words out before he exploded into uncontrollable fits of raucous laughter. No one round the table joined in though I only barely contained a nervous giggle. Colum seemed completely oblivious of our lack of merriment whilst John just sat there looking as if he was about to explode. We all felt paternal towards John, especially Rachel, so we all prayed that he'd come back with a witty riposte, but he just couldn't quite spit it out. I could see the cogs in his ever-logical brain desperately seeking a comeback but it wasn't happening. His inebriation would have presented no obstacle to working out some complex maths problem, but sharp-witted repartee had never been John's strong point.

I'd seen recurrences of this kind of interaction between Colum and John many times over the years. I don't know if Colum was simply a cruel bastard picking on the runt of the litter or whether there was something about John's autistic weirdness that wound him up, but no gathering of ours was complete without John's flushing scarlet as a result of Colum's ridicule. Once, John brought a girl to one of our parties at Cambridge and to say she wasn't exactly a looker would be a bit like saying that Joseph Merrick's modelling prospects weren't too hot. She was an overweight, spotty, lank-haired munter of the first order and Colum's mockery had been relentless and not overly subtle. He asked her whether she lived in Battersea, alluding to the dogs' home, and wondered aloud whether McDonald's or KFC was her favourite restaurant. At one point he began an earnest conversation about the merits of Clearasil and I even heard him talking about John being able to win 'dog of the night' for the rest of his life if he married her. John's fragile psyche was no match for Colum's vicious attacks and, although all of us at one time or another pleaded with Colum to be kinder, he remained merciless.

After about a minute of listening to Colum's unrestrained mirth I felt I had to say something so I came out with a time-tested cliché that I usually brought out at around 6 a.m. when everyone was so frazzled on booze and Class A that the audacity of its understatement occasionally garnered a few giggles.

'Come on, lads, we've all had a couple of drinks . . . let's not spoil it now.' A long pause. A funeral bell sounded mournfully some way off. A few tumbleweeds rolled by. I smirked nervously and lowered my head.

After yet more awkward silence Colum wiped the tears from his eyes and said: 'Sorry, lads . . . just couldn't help it.' There was no genuine remorse in his voice. John continued to sit there glaring at him, the veins in his temples throbbing as if he'd just taken a twenty-second snort of amyl nitrite. There was another uncomfortable silence but finally the usually taciturn Fergus chose to speak up.

'OK, well, I would certainly go along with John's suggestion. I can't think of anything I'd like to do more than hurt Geldlust . . . and banks in general, frankly. I think we'd all be doing the world a *big* favour if we punished those greedy *tossers* who have just got away with blue *fucking* murder. Paying each other huge bonuses after profiting from a fucking crisis *they* created which is destroying the lives of ordinary people everywhere. I'd string them all up . . . no offence, Steve.'

Oh, great; we had reached the inevitable stage in any knees-up when Fergus turned into a rabid Marxist-Leninist and started coating off bankers – temporarily forgetting that his best mate and girlfriend were stockbrokers. Usually I'd have Bridget to back me up, but . . . that wasn't the case this time, that would never be the case again. I banished that painful thought to the back of my mind and replied, 'Yeah, well . . . I'm not offended. You know I think they're all a bunch of ruthless wankers too and I'd love to fuck up Geldlust after what they did. I'm just working for the enemy for a few years to get a bit of cash under my belt and then I'll see you at the barricades, comrade! Consider me a sleeper agent . . . a fifth columnist ready to destroy the system from within.' I'd used this risible justification before; no one bought it then and no one bought it now. My lefty tendencies were genuine, I think, but it was always a little tricky claiming to be a socialist when I worked at the very heart of capitalism. It was one of the many contradictions that kept me up at night . . . that and my £300 a week coke habit.

'You see, Steve's right; he may be joking but we *do* have an inside agent within the very bank that caused Bridget's suicide.' John had snapped out of the furious silence that had occupied him since Colum's put-down. 'We can use him. What's more, all of us work in finance directly or indirectly. If we work together we can really hurt Geldlust.'

John's tones were becoming ever more excited. I could see Fergus's eyes light up. Rachel was listening intently. Colum, however, was staring at the perfectly formed rear of some barely legal chick standing at the bar and singing quietly to himself the immortal Motorhead lyrics: 'she's jailbait . . . and I can't wait.' After licking his lips with unrestrained lust he slowly turned round and, in a surprisingly lucid way, said:

'I know exactly how we can fuck 'em up . . . and make a few quid on the side.' We all stopped chatting and stared at him.

'Go on,' Fergus said.

Before the evening was out we'd all made a drunken pact to carry out Colum's scheme.

But I don't think any of us believed we'd actually do it . . .

I was flying through the air towards a rainbow. Stars and clouds whizzed past me. Suddenly I dipped and started heading to where the rainbow touched the ground. Forests and fields rushed by below me.

A little green-bearded fellow stood waiting in a field ahead of me. He beckoned me towards him. I could see a pot of gold by his side. I slowed down, touched my feet gently on the ground and walked towards him. When I was within a few feet, the leprechaun lifted up the pot's lid. I gingerly approached and stared within . . .

Inside was a white, old-fashioned telephone . . . and it was ringing.

It kept on ringing. A horrible annoying trill.

Slowly I roused myself out of my dream. My gummy eyes opened one at a time. My mouth tasted like a pub ashtray. My nostrils were red raw. My kidneys and liver felt like they'd gone twelve rounds with Mike Tyson. My dehydrated brain had shrunk to half its normal size and rattled around inside my cranium.

I wasn't dreaming. There was a bleeding phone ringing. My bleeding phone. Unfuckingacceptable. Who would dare do this on a Sunday morning? Why hadn't I turned it off? But those questions didn't stop the terrible ringing. I rooted around on the floor and found my suit trousers. Within their pockets lay the offending item. When I finally located it, I flirted with the idea of chucking it with all my force at the wall. Some annoyingly rational part of myself stopped me and I accepted the call.

It was Fergus. He sounded, as ever, amazingly together. He once claimed that he never had hangovers and nothing I'd ever witnessed belied his possession of that enviable quality, which I'd have given my right gonad to share.

'We're on. I've called the others. They'll all up for it and I already know you are. We're meeting at King's Cross next

Friday after work. Colum's booking us all rooms at a hotel in Cambridge – though of course he'll use false names. I'm really pleased you're on board.' He didn't wait for a response. He just hung up.

I hazily remembered the previous night's drunken commitment. That was no joke and this was no dream.

Oh shit.

Six

King's Cross
Friday, 26 November, 6 p.m.

WE ALL MET AT THE McDonald's by King's Cross station after work on Friday. The previous week at Geldlust had been unremittingly tedious and I had been woefully ineffectual. I'd had numerous sombre conversations with colleagues and clients alike and had even been pulled into Chris Browning's office for 'a chat about what happened'. This involved me staring at the ground whilst that snivelling dipshit came out with a bunch of meaningless platitudes about how sorry Geldlust was and how he had been very reluctant to sack Bridget but had been obliged to by Compliance, et cetera et cetera. I left his office having hardly said a word; to have shaken hands with him and politely agreed that Bridget's death had had nothing to with Geldlust would have made me feel like a filthy hypocrite.

Even exchanging those few words made me want to take a long, steaming hot bath.

During the week Fergus called almost every day. He had taken a week off work to make 'the preparations' for our 'off-site' which involved some serious research as well as regular probing chats with me. Communication with the other members of the group confirmed that he'd been in constant contact with them too – especially Colum. I'd never seen a man so committed to his self-appointed task. If he'd put the same energy into his journalistic career he'd have had a brace of Pulitzers weighing down his mantelpiece. He kept asking me for facts and figures about Geldlust and, at one point, even tried to persuade me to break into the office of the head of capital markets, Chris Browning's boss, and root around for some top secret documents. I had nipped that plan in the bud early doors but could tell that the matter was most certainly not closed. Fergus had the bit between his teeth and was not going to take no for an answer. The man was on a mission from God or whoever it was he took his orders from . . . maybe the other guy.

As each day passed I felt myself becoming more and more excited as well as increasingly apprehensive. A drunken plan in a pub after a highly emotional funeral was becoming ever more real with each passing hour. I tried to block the whole affair from my frazzled mind but attempting to do so only made me think about it all the more. I wasn't sleeping well and lived solely on takeaways and late-night TV. My colleagues kept commenting on my dishevelled appearance but I didn't care. I didn't bother to shave and showering had become less and less frequent. In the early hours I would wonder if we were really doing the right thing. Sure, I wanted revenge on Geldlust and felt that banks in general needed a serious slap in the face after what they'd just subjected the world to, but we were all going to face a shitload of trouble if we were caught. By the time we met at the McDonald's I was a bag of nerves. I strutted in a little late trying to look as tough and resolute as possible, knowing that the others would probably have already arrived. They had, and were chatting excitedly to each other, drinking McDonald's nutritious colas although only Colum had food in front of him – two Big Mac meals which had 'gone large'.

I arrived at the table, pointed at Colum's greasy gruel, half of which seemed to have been deposited on one of his chins, and innocently asked, 'Aren't we having a posh dinner tonight in Cambridge?'

Colum, speaking with a mouth full of reconstituted nostrils, simply said, 'I know, mate, but I needed a little something just to tide me over.' He certainly wasn't feeling nervous, but then he rarely did – or at least he always managed to conceal such beta male emotions from the rest of us.

We checked into our luxurious hotel under the false names we'd been allocated. Inevitably, Colum had selected 'Mike Hunt' for me purely so that he could con an unsuspecting Rachel into asking reception if 'anyone has seen Mike Hunt'. Even when Colum guffawed like a pub drunkard following her enquiry she was unaware that she'd been duped. She still didn't get it even after the receptionist began to giggle. At around 8.30 p.m., after a few sharpeners in the hotel bar, we headed out for some posh nosh in the private room of Quo Vadis – a cheeky little Italian restaurant we'd occasionally frequented when we were students.

Just before we started dinner Fergus tinkled his champagne flute with a fork and delivered a little speech. He was clearly uncomfortable taking centre stage even when amongst a small group of close friends, and I noticed that his voice had dropped an octave, which could have been because of his recent chain smoking . . . or maybe nerves.

'I just want to say that . . . I love you guys.' He put on a Glaswegian approximation of an American accent for the last four words. I suppose that doing so made it easier for him to openly express his emotions. We all laughed. 'These last two weeks have been almost unbearable for me, but with your help I've made it through. Instead of turning my attention from the oven to the razor blade and wondering which would do the job quicker I've focused on our . . . our project. We are going to do this thing and we're not just going to take vengeance on Geldlust, we're going to make a lot of money doing it too. I ask only two things. First, and this is particularly relevant for you, Colum, let's not get too drunk tonight; I want you thinking straight tomorrow. Second, let's not discuss the plan tonight . . . that's for tomorrow. What I'd like us to do this evening is just have a good time and remember what we all mean to each other and how much fun we have . . . or at least used to have. It's been too long since all five of us spent twenty-four hours together and it's great – look, for once, even Rachel has managed to get a pink ticket from her husband! Let's remember the good times gone and think about the good times coming.'

There was a polite round of applause and a few hearty 'hear, hear's from Colum . . . but suddenly Fergus's face darkened and I could see his eyes dampen. He swallowed hard and said in a croaky voice: 'Apart from that I just want to dedicate this project to the most wonderful woman I have ever met in my life . . . to Bridget. Let's raise a glass to Bridget.' Without a second prompting we all stood up round the table, clinked our glasses and said in unison 'To Bridget'. The stern faces of my friends reminded me of what we had lost and I too was forced to hold back the tears. Rachel didn't quite manage to do so and Colum put his bear-like arm round her shoulders to comfort her.

After that emotional start the evening progressed in a truly wonderful way. We talked and talked and talked – sometimes one on one with a neighbour and sometimes as a group. It felt like old times and everyone seemed relaxed and happy. A tiddly, giggling Rachel seemed elated to have secured a break from 'the fucking rug rats' and even John appeared relatively content. On several occasions he dared raise his voice and address the whole table and each time managed to garner more than just polite laughs.

Throughout the whole meal I found myself happily leaning back in my chair and surveying the scene. We had last all been in this room almost twenty years before when we had staged a raucous dinner party to celebrate finishing our finals. That affair had ended in a food fight and our getting kicked out by the proprietor who had told us never to darken his door again. Colum had responded to this affront by pulling his pecker out of his trousers and waving it at all the other diners within. For a brief moment, we were having fun – it was almost as if nothing had changed since our university days . . . except that one person was missing and her absence clawed at my heart every time I looked round the table.

Occasionally, however, I would catch Fergus looking around with an indecipherable expression on his face. It could have been either the content look of a man surrounded by his best friends or the uncomfortable glare of one who couldn't believe his pals were having such a good time so soon after losing someone so dear. But for the most part it was the sound of laughter that filled the air, especially when Colum held forth and told some of his oft-repeated anecdotes. He told us once again about the time he drunkenly drove into another car and, on seeing the driver call the police, parked and staggered off to the nearest off-licence where he bought a bottle of whisky, most of which he poured down the drain. When the police arrived and saw that he was so wasted that he could barely stand up straight Colum explained that he was 'of a nervous disposition' and had sought the solace of a stiff drink 'because the crash has properly freaked me out, ossifer'. He was found to be almost three times over the limit by the time they'd finally got him back to the station but when it later came to court, the judge, who heard confirmation of Colum's story from the off-licence's owner, let him off. Colum loved recounting this story for three simple reasons: it showed that he was a hard-drinking risk-taking muthafucker; it illustrated how street-smart he was even when off his nut; but most of all . . . because it was about Colum.

Despite Fergus's plea that we take things easy our teenage instincts inevitably got the better of us. It was simply impossible not to celebrate the gang's being together again, especially back in the town where we'd become friends. Ignoring our half-hearted protestations a highly inebriated Colum had paid for the whole meal with his black American Express card and insisted, as a quid pro quo, that we accompany him for a couple of snifters at a dreadful disco that we used to frequent called Ritzy's. It was one of the few clubs in central Cambridge and had been the scene of many a piss-poor evening when we'd been students. Rachel's twenty-first birthday party had taken place there in the last year of college and I'd famously passed out in its toilets for three hours after taking one too many smacky pills. Fergus had got into a fight with some local hard lads after they'd insulted Bridget there and John had been kicked out on more than one occasion for selling Ecstasy – in spite of the fact that what he was punting were in fact cat worming tablets that would have worked wonders on the innards of the chemical Sloanes who frequented the club. The place had been renamed and revamped but it was still reassuringly naff. There were lots of students shuffling around awkwardly and it was immediately obvious that the dancing skills of over-educated public school types hadn't improved one iota over the previous twenty years. Much to Fergus's displeasure Colum bought us all a few shots of tequila as soon as we entered and before you could say 'come on Granddad' we were all bopping around pretending not to nonce the young chicks. Colum of course approached several fresh-faced females but quickly received short shrift from his intended prey. I doubted they realised just what a lucky escape they'd had.

Still, we returned to the hotel at the surprisingly respectable hour of 1.30 a.m. and, after ignoring Colum's impassioned pleas that we have a last nightcap in the hotel bar, went straight to bed.

Everyone knew there was serious work to be done the next day.

'Gentlemen, what we propose is to undertake a classic bear raid . . .' said Fergus in his low, authoritative voice after we had moved from the breakfast room to the small hotel conference room Colum had booked. Fergus had quite clearly assumed leadership of the group and he was undoubtedly the best man for the job. Not only did his brief army training, imposing height and general Scottishness make him a naturally charismatic leader – this project was also his baby. He had put the energy into organising it and he had the strongest motivation to see it through. The rest of us were to some extent coming along for the ride. '. . . with a few extras thrown in for good measure. This, my friends, is going to be the most effective bear raid the world has ever seen.' His looked round the table into our eyes, nodding his head as he did so, hoping to convey the gravitas implied by his words.

'Before I go any further I have to confirm with each of you that you're up for this. It *is* illegal and we could get in a *lot* of trouble if we're caught – which shouldn't happen if we're smart. Still, if you not a hundred per cent committed to doing your bit in this project then you mustn't hear anything further about it. I'm going to go round the table and I want to hear a simple yes or no from each of you.'

He proceeded to look at each of us in turn and call out our name. All of us simply replied 'yes' though some, like Colum, said it far more confidently than others like John . . . or for that matter myself. Fergus was taking this shit really seriously and the more serious he was the higher my heart rate went.

'OK, that's good. I knew I could count on you guys. So I'm going to give a brief introduction and then I'm going to hand over to Colum – a man who, it turns out, has done this kind of thing several times before. I bet you were always wondering how come his hedge fund made so much money!'

Rachel, theoretically working for an organisation dedicated to preventing this kind of market abuse, burst into
giggles but, on seeing everyone else remain stony-faced,
stopped and turned bright pink. Meanwhile John scowled.
He'd probably always suspected that Colum's fund's stellar
performance had more to do with illegal trickery than its
boss's innate brilliance and now it was being confirmed.
Colum just sat there, a peculiar half-grin etched on to his
pink chubby face.

'First things first. I cannot emphasise strongly enough
how important secrecy is for us all. If this is to work and,
more important, if we are to get away with it, then no one
else must know anything about it – not even your husband,
Rachel. Even when we're talking to each other we must
ensure no one else can hear us.' Fergus was laying it on really
thick – I was beginning to think he'd seen one too many
films. 'So, on that subject we're going to give this plan a code
name . . . it's going to be called Operation Yogi . . . as in the
bear, geddit?' This time John let out a little giggle but was
quickly shut up by a stern glare from Fergus. We were
quickly getting the message that this was not the time for
laughter. 'We're also never going to talk about this to each
other on our current phones. I'm now going to give you each
a second-hand mobile fitted with an anonymous pay-as-you-
go SIM card with a hundred pounds of credit on it. There
are only *four* numbers saved in each phone – the new mobiles
of the other four members of the group. This phone is *never*
to be used to call anyone else . . . I don't care if your mum's

getting gang-raped by a pack of marauding gorillas, you are not to call anyone else, OK?' Fergus went round the table dishing out a disparate array of dodgy phones . . . 'Brick Lane's finest, my friend,' he smirked as he saw my look of horror on receiving some decade-old monstrosity. Once back at the front of the class he resumed his discourse.

'Finally, I've given you all code names. When calling each other or discussing the plan we *only ever* use these names. Colum and I had some fun coming up with them. They should be easy to remember as the first letter of the code name corresponds with the first letter of your Christian name.' Fergus allowed himself to grin at this point and Colum was beaming to himself, suppressing his giggles. I could tell we were about to be ridiculed. 'So, John . . . you're gonna be Jizz Stain.'

John raised his head and glared at Colum, flushing scarlet. '*No! No! No!* No fucking way! No fucking way!' His high-pitched voice combined with his repetition of the word 'no' made him sound robotic . . . like C-3PO being told he was gay by a Gamorrean Pig Guard. Colum was in hysterics, his head in his hands.

'Listen, John . . . none of these names are very flattering. This isn't *Reservoir Dogs* . . . we're all being called Mr Pink, OK?' John was still fuming but Fergus's natural authority quietened him down. 'OK, so Rachel, you're Ring Piece; Steve, you're Skid Mark; I'm Fuckwit and Colum is Cock Stick. You see, John? No one's "Mr Black", OK? Oh, and we'll call Geldlust Dog Shit PLC.' I could picture the giggles

Colum and Fergus had had thinking up our code names. I also saw the sense in what they were doing . . . trying to make light of a very serious situation. If we thought this was 'fun' it would be easier to make the whole thing out to be a bit of a school prank rather than a highly illegal project that could land all of us in the slammer.

'All right, so are you OK with that, Jizz Stain? Ring Piece? Skid Mark?' On receiving affirmative nods Fergus continued: 'Good, so that's settled. I'm gonna hand over to Colum . . . sorry, Cock Stick . . . who, with the help of some info given to us by Skid Mark, is going to explain exactly what we're going to do.' Fergus then sat down and laughed heartily – something I hadn't seen him do for weeks.

Colum stood up and turned on the laptop connected to the overhead projector. A graph showing three annotated share price charts popped up. My God, these boys were taking this seriously. They were treating the whole thing as a formal business presentation. We settled back in our chairs waiting to hear Cock Stick's pearls of wisdom.

'OK, so here's the deal.' There was a self-assured swagger, even in his tone of voice. 'I'm gonna give you the heads up on some blue sky thinking old Fergie and I have been doing. We've been thinking outside the box, and provided we sing from the same song sheet I reckon we should be able to get all our ducks in a row.' There was a stunned silence. This was the kind of meaningless management bullshit that we all hated. I couldn't believe that Colum was talking this way. Suddenly his face broke into a huge grin and he shouted:

'Gotcha, yer limey bastards!' and fell about laughing. After he'd got his guffaws under control he continued: 'No, but seriously . . . here before you are the share price charts of three major banks that you may have heard of: Lehmans, Bear Stearns and HBOS. The red arrows show where me and my compadres shorted the shares and the blue arrows show when we bought them back. I want you to know that from these three trades alone my firm made over two hundred million pounds and that some of the US boys in our group made over a billion dollars.' Colum waited for the enormity of his words to sink in. We all knew that he would have personally received around 10 per cent of that profit – around £20 million – from those three bets alone! No wonder he could afford his amazing penthouse apartment in Hoxton Square, a seven-bedroom mansion in Nice and a manor house in West Sussex with fifteen acres of land.

'I think most of you are familiar with the concept of the bear raid but, for John's benefit, I'll just briefly describe how it works.' John clenched and unclenched his fists a few more times. He seemed to spend most of his time doing that when Colum was around. 'You find a company that's vulnerable, and you and your mates sell short its shares and spread convincing rumours that it's going bust. Then you watch the share price plummet and the money roll in.'

Colum went on to describe how he and a bunch of 'great lads from across the pond' had been making coordinated bear raids on vulnerable financial firms for the last three years. It all sounded so easy, and Colum himself sounded totally confident when he said, 'My friends, if history teaches us anything it's that once you've lost the confidence of the market it's extremely difficult to win it back.' There had been a hell of a lot of rumours that this form of 'market manipulation' had been undertaken by dubious hedge funds during the financial crisis – especially in 2008 when things looked really precarious for the world economy. We were now hearing it straight from the horse's mouth. Colum gleefully admitted to helping exacerbate the credit crunch by spreading damaging rumours about various banks' financial viability. He was one of the devious bastards who sold short shares in the targeted firms just prior to making sure that their share prices kept dropping like a stone. He had actually helped bring down Lehmans, which in turn had ratcheted up the financial crisis by several notches. Of course, the rumours would have been irrelevant had the banks not got themselves in a right pickle in the first place, but there is no doubt that these lads had seriously worsened the situation. When the market is full of uncertainty, cleverly fabricated negative rumours can easily take root and lead to a vicious circle in which the decline of a bank's share price confirms that it must be in financial trouble, leading to further share price weakness, and so forth. If you're smart enough to have 'shorted' shares in the firm whose share price keeps dropping before this process gets going then you can end up making a shedload of wonga.

What Colum and his pals didn't even consider, of course, was that people lost their jobs, business failed and houses were repossessed from Shanghai to San Francisco as a result of their actions. The house of cards came tumbling down around them and they didn't give a rat's turd provided they kept coining it in. I almost couldn't believe how Colum's greed and selfishness had worsened over the years, or that he was still someone I considered a good friend.

Shorting shares is one of those things that 'civilians' generally don't understand, continued Colum. He really was preaching to the choir here but he was on a roll and no one bothered to explain that we all understood the concept of borrowing shares from a conventional pension or insurance fund and selling them on the stock market in the hope that they will subsequently drop in price. The idea is to buy back the shares at a lower price and return them to the fund they were borrowed from having picked up a tidy profit on the way. It's a high risk investment strategy and that's exactly why scurrilous hedge funds like to fix the game by spreading false rumours, using inside information and pulling other such tricks to help improve the odds on their bet, often working together in nefarious cabals to coordinate their attacks and, in so doing, help increase the likelihood of their punts coming good. Colum was clearly the happy member of one such group.

One thing was eminently clear from Colum's presentation – he was not remotely embarrassed about his role in helping to exacerbate the credit crunch. In fact, he seemed proud of it. After showing us how his group of conspirators had managed the trick on the 'test cases' of Lehmans and Bear

Geraint Anderson

Stearns (and a less successful attempt on HBOS that 'only' resulted in a 17 per cent one-day profit in April 2008) he went on to make several important points. First, that the financial climate was 'annoyingly' somewhat steadier now, which would make ruining Geldlust less easy. However, he had learnt a hell of a lot about how to undertake this kind of scheme from the ones he'd previously executed and we just needed to be a bit more 'inventive' to ensure that this one was 'a screaming success'. Fortunately, he had also learnt a lot about the exotic financial products that can make a bear raid extra profitable. Finally, he felt sure that with the talent sitting right there in the room there'd be no significant obstacle to untold riches for all.

He then looked me straight in the eye and said: 'And, of course, we have our inside man, Skid Mark!' He stifled a giggle. 'He doesn't know it yet but he's going to be doing a spot of burglary and a little bit of cyber crime for us to make sure we all come out of this smiling.' Everyone turned to stare at me. I felt like protesting but could already see that I had no choice. Fuck . . . it was going to be me taking the biggest risk.

The rest of the presentation involved pie charts and block graphs showing Geldlust's various financial liabilities and its position relative to other banks on several different metrics – tier one ratios, gross assets, return on equity and so forth. Colum was using publicly available information from Geldlust's annual report as well as some facts I had gleaned from a few confidential internal documents I'd

98

managed to get my grubby mitts on over the previous week. At the end we were all given a timeline describing exactly what each one of us needed to do and when. We all had our roles and, if things went smoothly, it looked like a pretty damn good plan. Colum told us that, taking into account the more buoyant economic environment, he would consider a 20 to 25 per cent share price decline to be a resounding success. Of course, we would use financial derivatives to make our upside a massive multiple of that number.

By this time there was a real buzz in the air and everyone was smiling. For the first time in years, there was a wonderful feeling of unity amongst us. We felt like a genuine bunch of bank robbers planning the next big job. And it *was* a 'bank job' . . . just a different kind: the kind that didn't require getaway cars and guns; the kind that could, if it worked well, make us tens of millions . . . oh, and avenge Bridget's death, of course.

That's when I started to question why exactly we were doing this. There didn't seem to be a singular motive any more. Was it revenge for Bridget? It clearly was for Fergus and to some extent for us all, but Bridget had hardly been mentioned all day. Was it some lefty urge to pay the banks back for their crimes against humanity? It definitely was for John, Fergus and maybe even me, but Colum and Rachel had no truck with what they called CSB or 'Champagne Socialist Bullshit'. Was it just to make a fast buck? Certainly for Colum, who cared about little else, but maybe that was the real spur to action for us all . . . excluding perhaps

Fergus. And there were other motivations too. I knew that Rachel had hated Geldlust ever since she'd been fired by its executives two years before. I also knew that John had a massive chip on his shoulder about investment banks generally, and Geldlust in particular. He hated being pushed into poor-performing shares by traders offloading some dreadful stock that had been festering on their books for months. He also detested corporate finance departments conning him into investing in horseshit IPOs, and Geldlust was very au fait with both these practices. But most of all he despised the arrogant pinstriped toffs who populated investment banks, who had got their jobs purely through family connections, had thrived due to the misplaced self-assurance they fed you with your milk at public school, and earned five times as much as he did even though he was so much smarter than them. It would be a pleasure for John to take those cocksure, chinless tosspots down a peg or two.

And as for me . . . well, for me it was, I suppose, a bit of everything – all of the above, if you like. I'd always hated my job and had been horrified by the banks' despicable and unpunished crimes of the previous decade. I particularly hated Geldlust for its treatment of Bridget . . . and, well, the money most certainly wouldn't go amiss. It also felt great to be part of the gang again. The previous night had reminded me of how lonely I'd become recently. Things had changed so much since my return from my forced absence from Britain a couple of years before. I'd seen less of my oldest friends Fergus and Bridget as a result of their relationship.

I'd ceased hanging out with John who'd become increasingly weird and reclusive. Rachel's parenting duties and her dull husband had ensured that I rarely saw her, and Colum's 900-mile-an-hour lifestyle had become less appealing as I approached the big 4-oh. No, I'd spent the last year or two on my own or hanging out with a bunch of interchangeable acquaintances pretending to have a great time. It was going to be wonderful re-establishing relations with my real friends. Yeah, that was probably the most important thing . . . actually connecting with people rather than just floating along wondering where it had all gone wrong.

It would also be a laugh to see if we could actually pull this off; to make the headlines and shake the system up a bit.

Of course, the last thing it turned out to be was a laugh.

Part Two

Part Two

'When I find a short-seller, I want to tear his heart out and eat it before his eyes while he's still alive' – Dick Fuld Jr, former CEO and Chairman of Lehman Brothers, in 2008, just before his firm went bust and sent the global economy into a tailspin.

Seven

EVEN AT THIS LATE HOUR, there were still a few hard-working spods on the trading floor. I couldn't believe that these soulless dorks were still at it and wondered what the hell they were up to. The head of sales, Chris Browning, had left over an hour ago so it wasn't as if their diligence was going to be noticed and taken into account when B-day came round. Maybe these knobs actually liked sitting in a huge open-plan office learning pointless horseshit, or perhaps their home life was so unremittingly dreadful that they preferred to lounge around composing spreadsheets rather than endure another silent dinner with a moody wife who was probably porking her tennis coach. Since I usually left work on the dot of 6 p.m. I'd already received a few confused looks from my more industrious colleagues. A couple of smarmy dickheads had made some jokey comments about my new-found conscientiousness as they passed me on their way out, which I had soundly ignored. Little did these losers know that I wasn't here to hone up my knowledge of the French pharmaceutical industry or refresh my memory about how to calculate the weighted average cost of capital. Oh no, I was here to do something far more interesting . . .

As it approached 8 p.m. I decided to make my move. A few more of the lads had left and there was now a clear run to the corridor leading to Chris's office. I knew he never locked it and I knew where he kept the key to his filing cabinet. Two months before he had taken it out of the top right-hand drawer of his desk in front of me when retrieving some correspondence he'd had with the overall head of Geldlust – the big cheese back in Frankfurt – in response to concerns I had raised regarding Geldlust's continued commitment to its equity division. Some rumours had been circulating in the financial press that Geldlust's CEO, Herr Herman Pfister (aka 'the Pfist of Fury' or 'Herman ze German' as our ever-humorous traders imaginatively called him), was undertaking a strategic review and that Geldlust's underperforming investment banking arm was on the chopping block. Obviously, this hadn't instilled any of us with much confidence about the longevity of our careers and a few of my fellow salesmen had nominated me to go and ask Chris about it. After I'd explained our worries, Browning had reached into his filing cabinet and removed a letter to him and various other investment banking MDs from 'ze German'. It actually wasn't that reassuring because, predictably, there was nothing in writing that confirmed our division's continued existence. It recognised that there had been 'unfounded damaging rumours' and admitted that there were 'unexpected knock-on effects from the sub-prime crisis' but went on to say that Geldlust remained dedicated to investment banking. Of course, this statement was preceded by lots of caveats including one about Frankfurt's commitment being contingent on 'there being no materially adverse changes in market conditions'. So basically it said bugger all – which is exactly what I reported back to Big Al and the lads, some of whom immediately called up their favourite headhunters.

After a few deep breaths I strolled as casually as possible towards the coffee machine that was situated at the beginning of Chris's corridor. I nervously punched in the code for a café latte; a white plastic cup clattered into place and some foul-smelling black goo began pouring into it. After a nonchalant look around I darted into the corridor. My heart rate had gone up several notches and I felt beads of sweat trickling down between my shoulder blades. I marched down the corridor, pleased to see that none of the glass-fronted offices were occupied, and after ten metres arrived at Chris's door. After a final glance behind me I pushed down on the handle and entered. I noticed that my hand was shaking. Closing the door as quietly as possible, I rushed behind Chris's desk and opened the right-hand drawer. It took me a moment to locate the key amongst a pile of paper clips and rubber bands, and seconds later the filing cabinet was open. My heart was really pumping now. I couldn't stop myself looking back at the door every few seconds, half expecting some security guard to walk in at any moment.

Much to my relief it was clear that Chris had filed everything in a very anal way – which was no surprise taking into account his play-it-by-the-book modus operandi. I quickly found and removed the file titled *Correspondence with Pfister* and started leafing through it. Within about a minute I had found four letters from the Pfist of Fury on the CEO's headed paper with his signature at the bottom, as well as some emails from him that Chris had printed out. I was pleased to see that several of them discussed Geldlust's potential exposure to certain dubious financial derivatives and Pfister's minor concerns about various off-balance-sheet special purpose vehicles that had invested heavily in mortgage-backed securities as well as Greek and Portuguese government bonds that some were beginning to say were not worth the paper they were written on. They all had the word *Confidential* stamped at the top. I folded the letters up and put them in my inside jacket pocket. I then locked the filing cabinet, replaced the key and walked back to the coffee machine as if nothing had happened. I carried the rank liquid purporting to be café latte shakily back to my desk, trying my damnedest to suppress the huge smile that desperately wanted to spread itself over my face.

After a short wait pretending to work on my computer I headed off to Fergus's flat. He had all the equipment we needed for the next part of the plan . . .

Geldlust Investment Bank
Tuesday, 30 November, 12.15 p.m.

I pulled up the spreadsheet of my current investments on my computer screen. It wasn't a pretty sight. Like most stockbrokers I had tended to 'invest' my hard-earned cash not in solid blue-chip FTSE 100 companies but rather in crap penny shares that could either increase tenfold in value or go bust. Unfortunately, during the market turmoil of the previous three years many had opted for the latter option, leaving me with a bunch of pestilent dogs. Despite the obvious risks brokers often end up pursuing this 'investment strategy' because we are all too aware that blue-chip companies like Marks & Spencer or British Airways are so thoroughly analysed by 'experts' that being able to spot an angle that the market had not already factored into the share price is generally harder than finding a fourteen-year-old virgin in Solihull. Hence, we listen to piss-poor tips from half-cut traders at sleazy titty bars and often find ourselves with a portfolio composed of utter horseshit and the odd share that is worth ten times what we'd paid for it. Still, I had bought the occasional sensible share when markets across the globe were having their arses soundly kicked in

Geraint Anderson

Q1 2009. Now that the markets had recovered somewhat I owned about £150,000 worth of shares in Barclays, HBOS and Royal Sun Alliance, which would all have to go. No financial company was going to remain unaffected by Geldlust's upcoming trials. I had also accrued around £250,000 worth of Geldlust shares via my bonses, though only a third of this was accessible; most of it would vest over the following two years. I'd just have to take that potential hit on the chin and make sure the profits I made from Geldlust's imminent turmoil more than outweighed it. That was unlikely to be a problem, especially as Colum had promised to give each of us 2 per cent of the profit his hedge fund made from Geldlust's looming share price decline. That's where we'd make the real money. If his fund made £200 million, as he hoped, then we'd all make around £4 million each, though this was, of course, nothing compared to what Colum would pocket.

After some thought, I also decided to cash in all the dodgy shares I'd accrued. Many of these small, illiquid companies could suffer badly if our actions brought about any kind of temporary return to the credit crunch. They generally had fewer reserves to eat into, so if bank lending were to dry up there was a chance they could face bankruptcy. I suddenly felt pangs of guilt as I realised that our scam could end up losing people jobs at dodgy internet firms in Reading and gas storage businesses in Scotland but quickly dismissed them; surely our little prank wouldn't have such far-reaching consequences.

In order to sell any 'PA shares' (personal account shares) at an investment bank you have to check two things. First, whether the stock is covered by one of your analysts; if it is you need to show the compliance department a signed document from the relevant analyst stating that he or she is not going to publish a price-sensitive note about that specific stock for at least three days. Second, you have to check the firm's intranet to make sure that the company is not on your bank's 'restricted list', which comprises all those companies the bank may have some minor corporate interest in. If the toffee-nosed Etonians up on the tenth floor thought there was even a sniff of a chance of issuing some bonds for a company or playing some minor role in an upcoming acquisition it may make, then we weren't allowed to trade its shares. The fact that 90 per cent of these schemes never came to fruition for a two-bit operation like Geldlust was an irrelevance as far as our compliance boys were concerned. I scanned the intranet and found that only one of my dodgy penny shares was on the restricted list. Seeing that my stake in it had reduced in value by 76 per cent since I had so wisely acquired it, I wasn't overly bothered. I then spent the next half an hour up on the research floor collecting signatures off the bespectacled boffins who had once been my working companions. I exchanged polite 'hello's, but neglected to mention that I'd be spending the next week or two doing my damnedest to destroy the company they toiled night and day for.

I then went to see the compliance trolls on the fourth floor. I was hoping to locate some junior muppet who would simply rubber stamp my proposed trades, no questions asked, and when a secretary buzzed me in I made for the desk of a little squit I'd had dealings with before. I was just about to lay my signed documents in front of him for his counter-signature when I heard my name. Richard Stimp had scuttled out of his office immediately on seeing me and, with a crooked forefinger and a malicious grin, was beckoning me towards his domain. I was in his kingdom now and he was not going to forgo this opportunity to push his weight around. My shoulders slumped, and I approached him knowing full well that I was going to receive a tirade of sarcastic bullshit.

'So, Steve . . . how can we help you?' Even the people seated ten desks away would have picked up the sneer in his tone. I could sense my hackles rising.

'Hi, Richard. Just cleaning up my PA portfolio a little,' I said wearily. I handed him the eight signed documents permitting me to sell my shares. My heart sank as he strolled back into his office with them. I followed him in, dragging my feet behind me like a naughty schoolboy about to receive a severe telling-off. He sat down behind his desk and proceeded to examine each document in minute detail. He licked his thumb and forefinger and slowly leafed through them, relishing his momentary power over me, before starting up his computer and checking the intranet to see if any of the shares were on the restricted list.

After an annoyingly long pause he looked up at me and sneered: 'So, that all looks in order. But tell me, why are you so keen to sell all these shares? What do you know that the market doesn't, eh?' He actually had no right to ask that question but I didn't want to respond angrily in case it raised his suspicions. Instead I would utilise the fine art of talking codshit – something fourteen years of broking had honed into second nature.

'Well, I'm not sure if you're aware of this, but Morgan Stanley went negative on the market last week and Citigroup issued a note yesterday saying that the post-credit crunch bull market has run its course. I think that when two such heavyweights change their opinion only an idiot wouldn't stand up and take notice.' I spat out the word 'idiot' hoping Richard knew exactly who I was referring to. That part of the crap was real but the next bit was steaming horse manure of the highest order. 'Combine those concerns with the fact that I'm thinking of moving house and you can see why I'm cashing in a few stocks.'

'But I thought you'd moved house only a few months ago?' Richard said, his eyes narrowing suspiciously. Now this was true, but there was no reason to expect Richard would have known about it. It was becoming apparent that the officious little creep had been keeping close tabs on my every move.

'Erm, that's right, but . . . I'm thinking about buying another property and renting out the first one.' I suddenly decided that I'd had enough of his interrogation. 'Anyway,

Richard, what I'm doing with my cash has got fuck all to do with you so, unless you see a problem with the paperwork, I think this conversation is over.' I desperately wanted to keep my cool despite feeling my blood boil. This nasty little twat had Bridget's blood on his hands.

'Well, it does all seem OK . . . though I can't say I'm not disappointed that you're selling all the Geldlust shares you're allowed to. Think we're facing rocky times, eh?' There was a pseudo-friendliness in his voice as if he imagined I was going to 'fess up to him about some insider knowledge. The little prick must have thought it was fucking amateur night.

'No, Richard, I don't – I just need the cash, OK?' And with that I grabbed the papers from his desk and stormed out of his office. I could feel my face turning puce with anger – something I really didn't want Richard to see. I wasn't just angry at him; I was angry with myself for doing something that might have put him on the alert. I realised that I should have just forfeited my Geldlust equity for the greater good, but some tight-arse part of me couldn't face owning £80,000 worth of shares that I knew were likely to get their backsides soundly kicked over the coming weeks. As I had a furious piss in the gents I decided not to tell the others about my little contretemps with Richard . . . there was no point in worrying them unnecessarily.

Liverpool Street
Wednesday, 1 December, 2.15 p.m.

'No, Auntie Marge, there's nothing dodgy about this, I promise you. It's simply a legitimate way for me to avoid capital gains tax.'

'What's that then, Steve?' she asked as if I'd just mentioned some obscure element of quantum physics. I took a long, deep breath.

'OK, so, you know that we're all allowed to make around ten grand of capital gains each year tax free?' I was pacing around Exchange Square chatting away on my mobile trying to avoid the scurrying bankers who had popped out of their offices to buy a lunchtime sandwich.

'No, to be honest, love, I haven't a clue what you're talking about.' Aunt Marge's Welsh accent down the mobile made the whole conversation more comical than it already was. It was as strong as ever despite the fact she'd lived in Ealing for the best part of twenty years.

'OK, if I buy some shares and sell them a few weeks later and make a twenty-thousand-pound profit I have to pay lots of tax on half of that profit . . .'

'Did you do that, Steve, really? Oh, there's lovely . . . you always were such a clever boy.' Aunt Marge and my other older Welsh relatives and all their friends still referred to me as 'boy', or sometimes 'bach', despite the fact that I was thirty-eight and earning more in a year than they probably had in their whole lifetime. I was not offended by this but actually found it strangely reassuring.

'No . . . I did not do that. However, I suspect that this next investment is going to be a sure-fire winner and I'm concerned that the tax man is going to try to grab some of my winnings. So, what I thought I'd do is meet you down in Ealing this evening and set you up a few spread betting accounts and an online stockbroking account. I'll then hand you over thirty grand in cash to put into your bank account tomorrow morning. I'll come back tomorrow lunchtime and we'll place the bets . . . I mean investments.'

'Thirty thousand pounds? My God, bach, I've never seen that kind of money. But if you promise me this is all above board then I'll do it for you. I only wish your uncle Gareth was here to help me – he always had a knack when it came to money.' The beauty of Auntie Marge was that she wasn't a blood relative, which made the chances of some diligent FSA wanker looking into her share dealings highly unlikely.

I ended the call, having once again reassured Marge that it was all kosher, and walked back to the office. It had been my fifth and final such conversation that lunchtime organising my side bets on Geldlust. I'd selected a couple of old school friends and three distant relatives, all of whom lived in London. They were sensible, law-abiding citizens who, more importantly, I knew wouldn't ask me for too much commission. They'd all been surprisingly cool about the whole thing, though I suppose my promise to give them 10 per cent of any profit we made combined with the fact it was my money that was being put at risk had proved quite an attractive offer.

In order to avoid any kind of paper trail I had to give them the money cash in hand, which was a little difficult considering the fact that together they required £150,000. However, I had planned ahead and used a variety of bank accounts to withdraw the money over the previous days. I also had a list of pre-allocated spread betting companies that Fergus and Colum had handed out during our 'off-site', three of whom I was allowed to use. Geldlust's shares were trading on average at around €54 when I got my five selected pals to use the £30,000 I'd given them to bet against my bank. On my instruction, they all sold Geldlust shares at between £3,000 and £7,000 a point, which would mean that every euro Geldlust's share price fell would give me a profit of approximately £45,000. Not bad for pushing around a few bits of paper and certainly better than working for a living.

I had about £180,000 left in my bank accounts which I decided to invest in gold, which everyone piles into whenever markets face tricky times. If we were as successful as I thought we might be then the price of gold was likely to rise perhaps 6 to 7 per cent. I logged on to my online broker and bought three-month gold futures 4 per cent above the current price of $1,375 a troy ounce. If the gold price hit $1,450 within the next month then I'd almost double my money.

It took several days to finish all my personal financial

preparations and a few short coded conversations with Fuckwit, Cock Stick and the rest of the crew confirmed that by Friday they were all sorted too.

Now I just had to get through a lonely weekend with only a few bottles of claret and Mr Tibbs for company, and then Operation Yogi proper would begin.

There'd be no partying, but I still doubted I'd sleep a wink.

Eight

Provincial Mutual Insurance offices, Cornhill
Monday, 6 December, 11.05 a.m.
(Geldlust share price €53.7)

'WE CAN'T JUST LIQUIDATE OUR entire two per cent stake in Geldlust in a matter of days. That's not the way we do things at Provincial Mutual . . . we invest for the long term.' The weekly investment committee meeting at John's fund management firm had got off to an unusually heated start. John had warned the four other senior FMs three days before that he had a radical proposal but there was still an initial stunned silence when he'd opened proceedings by saying that Provincial Mutual should immediately dump its entire stake in one of their key financial holdings. His boss, a bushy-eye-browed, cauliflower-nosed pisshead called Sir William Masterful, had interrupted him even before he could explain his reasoning, and the other FMs were nodding in sycophantic agreement. Nodding especially hard was John's office enemy Angela Trout who, by a cruel twist of fate, had grown to resemble her namesake. Of course John had expected opposition, but persuading these brain-dead dingbats was now looking likely to prove a little harder than he'd hoped. He was going to have to pull out all the stops and deliver a truly bravura performance.

'Sir William, I don't just think we *should* liquidate our Geldlust position . . . I think we have no choice but to liquidate it.' John's fervour, combined with the radical nature of his proposal, made sure that everyone in the old wood-panelled room was, for once, hanging on his every word.

'But what's the rush? If we are to sell, which you still need to convince us of, why don't we do it over a few weeks so as to minimise the impact on the share price?' asked Angela, whose nasal tones and shoe-size IQ made John wince every time she spoke. John could barely accept that 'the Trout' and he shared job titles . . . in fact, he could barely accept that she was a member of the same species, let alone the same profession. His reply was slow and he enunciated each word carefully as if he were talking to a Cornish village idiot.

'We have to sell because Geldlust is due to give its end-of-year trading statement on 17 December and I have no doubt that what they say then will cause the share price to fall between thirty-five and forty per cent.' John paused to allow the significance of his words to sink in and then continued: 'I also happen to know that several major hedge funds are planning to build a position in the stock over the next few days because of some takeover rumours – which are completely spurious because the State of Saxony owns a controlling twenty-five per cent stake and would rather buy the whole thing back than let some foreign bank take it over. This near-term buying should offset our selling and is *only* going to be taking place this week.' John's usually monotonous voice was cracking with emotion. The other FMs had never seen him so impassioned about his job. Then Angela piped up.

'And you're pretty sure Geldlust is going down?'

'Look, my own fund owns point four per cent of Geldlust and I shall be selling it all over the next three days. I'm not just "pretty sure" about this, I'm totally convinced. In fact, I'd stake my annual bonus on it.' John looked at each of the other FMs in turn. He knew that this kind of macho talk was more suited to some big-swinging-dick hedge fund and that he was overplaying his hand at this sleepy mutual, but he didn't care. He had to put a rocket up these stiffs' flabby arses if he was to play his vital role in Operation Yogi.

'OK, OK. Let's calm down, gentlemen . . . oh, and, erm, and Angela,' stuttered Sir William, who was ever aware of his mustachioed ancestors hanging on the wall looking down at him disapprovingly for employing a woman. 'So you've explained how and when we should sell our shares; now please convince us . . . *why*.' He sat back creakily in his green leather-backed chair, pleased with the resonance that the elongated last word of his sentence had produced. He had been head of Provincial Mutual for almost twenty years and had taken over the firm from his father. He loved his job, mainly because it involved rolling into work at about 10 a.m., a boozy three-hour gourmet lunch with some of his ex-Harrow banker chums and then a quiet afternoon snooze in his plush office.

John stood up and strode confidently towards the front of the conference room. He had left behind his usual nervous demeanour and had turned into a mean, clean investing machine. For once he felt strong and powerful, a wolf amongst sheep. He dimmed the lights and switched on the laptop attached to the overhead projector. Immediately, a bar chart appeared comparing Geldlust's exposure to sub-prime mortgages as a proportion of its revenues and its market capitalisation with those of the other major banks. He then proceeded to give an extremely persuasive present-ation featuring graphs and obscure details garnered from the annual reports, as well as some false statistics that showed very clearly that Geldlust's management had used clever accounting to underplay its liabilities.

At the end of his ten-minute diatribe everyone on the committee, apart from Angela, looked suitably impressed. She had a natural aversion to making any radical moves like the one proposed by John and had never liked the too-clever-by-half little upstart anyway. She had noted his condescension over the previous years and had been irritated by him several times when he had publicly exposed her atrocious grasp of equity valuation techniques. She was an old-school fund manager who based her investment decisions on broker tips, me-too momentum trading and some nebulous get-out-of-jail-free card called 'market savvy', otherwise known as inside information. She often dismissed John's advice and tried to get the others on the committee to do the same by claiming he had the market feel of 'a teenage day trader'.

After staring at John for a few seconds she piped up: 'John, you know that I respect your opinions enormously' – that was her first obvious lie – 'and that I am a strong believer in fundamental valuation' – that was her second – 'but if this information is in the public domain then surely the twenty or so eager beaver sell-side analysts out there would have noticed that something was amiss?' It was actually a surprisingly incisive question for Angela, but fortunately John had prepared himself for just such a query. He pulled out the ace he'd been keeping up his pinstriped sleeve.

'Yes . . . well, some information has been made available to me . . . some information that isn't necessarily in the public domain . . .' John looked round at his colleagues for confirmation that he was allowed to go ahead and give them some blatantly illegal inside information. Whilst all of Provincial Mutual's senior FMs occasionally engaged in insider trading it was rare to openly indicate that you did so. There was a suitably long pause as John's colleagues stared at their laps waiting for Sir William's reaction. Eventually he rubbed his swollen purple nose and broke the silence.

'Yes, well . . . go on.'

That was all the prompting John needed. He proceeded to pass around four letters from Dr Pfister to Chris Browning – all of which were headed up with the words *Highly confidential*. Sir William read the first one with growing astonishment, his rheumy eyes widening with every sentence.

Highly confidential
2 December 2010

Dear Chris,
I'm writing to inform you that the situation we spoke about five days ago has materially worsened. It is now clear that Geldlust has far greater liabilities associated with the US sub-prime mortgage situation than has been publicly declared. It appears that certain bankers working in structured finance had created off-balance-sheet vehicles that are now deeply in the red and were not picked up by the auditors. None of these losses have been reported in our accounts. Combine these liabilities with several €500m+ losses made by three rogue traders and you can appreciate that we face a *very* serious problem. Whilst it is currently impossible to precisely calculate the losses related to these issues, our nearest estimate is €5 to 6bn i.e. almost half our market value. These matters have come to our attention over the last week and we have little choice but to mention them at our

pre-closed season trading statement of 17 December. The likely market reaction will be brutal and there is even a chance of a Lehmans/Bear Stearns situation if we cannot reassure the market convincingly.

Yours sincerely,

Dr Herman Pfister

The letters had, of course, all been suitably doctored by Colum and Fergus to make out that Geldlust was in truly dire straits. A word processor, a pair of scissors, some Tippex and a photocopier were all that were required to produce almost perfect fake letters with genuine signatures at the bottom. Colum and Fergus had then photographed the newly produced letters with a spy camera they'd acquired from a surveillance shop in Covent Garden. The lettering was at an angle and a little blurry which just added to the documents' authenticity. They now looked as though they'd been uncovered by a daring James Bond-style industrial espionage mission and those who were lucky enough to see them had genuine gold dust in their hands. John could see his colleagues looking ever more shocked as they passed the letters between them. Finally, Sir William spoke up, coughing his embarrassment at so clear a breach of the law: 'And, ahem, where did you, ahem, acquire these documents?'

'I'm not at liberty to name my source but I will say this about her. She works closely with several of the Geldlust MDs, I completely trust her and she has no reason to dupe us.'

He went round the room collecting the false documents he'd just dished out. As he gathered the last of the letters he smiled to himself. He knew that were the shit to hit the fan none of his colleagues would say that it was he who had conned them into selling their shares – to do so would be to tacitly admit that they had acted on what they thought was genuine inside information.

After John sat down Sir William cleared his throat again. 'Well, in my thirty years on the market I can think of few more obvious trades than this one. I just wish we were a hedge fund and could short the bastard. So before you all bugger off I think we should agree that Provincial Mutual's entire Geldlust stake should be offloaded over the next two days. Do we agree?' It was more like a statement than a question. Unsurprisingly, everyone raised their hand and nodded.

'Good. I shall instruct our trader to earn his salt and get us out of this dog as quickly and efficiently as possible, starting tomorrow afternoon.' With that Sir William headed off to his first extended lunch of the week, but not before patting John on the shoulder and muttering, 'Good work, young man, good work.'

Forty-five minutes later John walked out of his office towards the Pret A Manger he frequented nearly every lunchtime. On the way over he took out the cheap and nasty mobile from his inside pocket and selected the number of his least favourite of the four 'friends' saved within.

'Hello, Cock Stick. It's . . . Jizz Stain.' He heard a loud, all-too-familiar laugh on the other end of the phone, and gritted his teeth. 'Phase one has gone very smoothly and by the end of Wednesday we will no longer hold any shares in Dog Shit plc. We start selling tomorrow afternoon and the price will begin to fall appreciably. Please inform Ring Piece and Skid Mark.'

Colum grinned to himself. The scam would have been worth doing just to hear John say that last sentence alone.

'Well, good luck then.' John was desperate to not be on the phone to his old nemesis any longer than was strictly necessary.

'Baby, I don't need it,' was Colum's simple reply.

Now it was down to business. He'd spent all morning at his plush Mayfair office leaning back in his £4,000 ergonomically designed black leather chair with his feet on his desk spreading a false rumour to his fellow hedge fund managers and any brokers who happened to call him up that Geldlust was about to be acquired by 'a large US bank at a 30 per cent premium'. He was a respected and trusted City player whose fund's stellar performance was the envy of many. Hence, his words of wisdom were spreading like wildfire down phone lines and via emails. After John's call he pulled up Geldlust's stats on one of the six screens in front of him and smiled to himself when he saw that an unusually large amount of buying was pushing up volumes as well as Geldlust's share price. It was only halfway through the day yet over eleven million shares had been traded and Geldlust's share price was up 2.7 per cent. The massive buying would make it easier to short the shares without pushing the price down. It also meant that Geldlust's upcoming decline would be all the more severe – especially when Colum 'suddenly realised' the next day that the State of Saxony was never going to be willing to sell its controlling stake in a month of Sundays.

Colum leant back in his chair, smiled, and folded his chunky arms behind his head. He'd wait until Reuters, Bloomberg and the Tuesday morning newspapers had, with his help, got hold of the takeover story before he started phase two of the plan.

Everything was going swimmingly.

Nine

Alpha Max Hedge Fund, Mayfair
Tuesday, 7 December, 8.15 a.m.
(€57.8, up 4.8% on the day)

OLUM PARKED HIS BRIGHT RED 1200CC Ducati Diavel Carbon motorbike in the scooter bay directly in front of his office. Despite the heavy rush-hour traffic he had made the journey from Hoxton in under twelve minutes, weaving through static cars like Barry Sheene after a three-day crystal meth bender. He removed his helmet, and with a film of noxious sweat covering his pink, chubby face walked up the six steps to what looked like just any other five-storey Georgian house in Mayfair. On reaching the seemingly anonymous front door he pressed the bell marked *Alpha Max*. His receptionist Sharon, a stunning blonde from Wandsworth with the voluptuous body of a seventies porn star, buzzed him in. One of Colum's key decisions when setting up Alpha Max six years before had been, as he'd gleefully told Fergus, that 'any woman working here has to make me wanna cream my jeans', with their secretarial skills playing a very distant second fiddle to that main requirement. This did mean that certain hires had been farcically incompetent but Sharon had proved to be one of the better ones; she even knew how to type. Sharon was also fully aware of Colum's unconventional selection process and so spent over thirty minutes every morning dolling herself up. It was a worthwhile investment; last year Colum had given her a 'discretionary bonus' of £50,000 and it certainly wasn't for her shorthand skills. Unfortunately, Sharon was married, and despite constant flirtation on Colum's part had, so far, proved to be one of the few secretaries he hadn't persuaded to give him a hasty nosh in the toilets. The ever-present possibility that this might occur had helped ensure that she kept her job and Colum had frequently been heard to say to his City pals over a glass or six of Dom Perignon that it was 'a question of when, not if, the little tart gets on her hands and knees'.

Colum wheezed his way up one flight of stairs and into the office of the company that had made him a multi-multi-millionaire. He'd cut his teeth at quality hedge funds for eight years before striking out on his own and, helped by his willingness to break rules, had delivered an average annual return of 22 per cent to his investors. In his world this was truly magnificent and had attracted an influx of cash from Russian oligarchs and oil-rich Arabs as well as several scary Mafia types whose sullen visits Colum always dreaded.

Alpha Max now ran over £1 billion and MD Colum personally received 10 per cent of any performance that the fund achieved above the yield of a gilt – a farcically low hurdle rate considering that interest rates were now close to zero. Another 10 per cent of any outperformance was split up amongst Colum's five junior partners whom he got to do all his grunt work. Colum kept his illegal 'investment techniques' to himself but all his colleagues were savvy enough to realise that his extraordinary ability to consistently guess which companies were about to be taken over or issue profit warnings did not result from being a dab hand with the tarot cards or having Mystic Meg on speed dial. The ever-effective FSA had sniffed around a couple of times after he'd piled into Boots and Cadburys merely a day before they'd announced that they were in 'takeover talks that may or may not lead to an offer', but, as usual, he had simply been able to claim that he'd been 'extremely jammy'. Since they had not heard or recorded the mobile phone calls from his contacts in the corporate finance departments of the investment banks that were organising the acquisitions they had no proof, and once again he was able to laugh all the way to the bank – unlike the dumbass pension funds who had unwittingly sold him their stock just before it sky-rocketed.

'Good morning, Mr Boyd, and may I say that you are looking exceedingly sexy in your biker leathers today?' said Sharon, fluttering her heavily made-up eyes as she did so. This was her standard way of welcoming her debauched boss.

'Thank you, Sharon. You're not looking too scruffy yourself. You know, I should take you for a ride one day . . . wouldn't you like to have something big and red throbbing between your legs?' Colum had used this piss-poor gag numerous times before and Sharon always laughed obediently. In most offices such a comment could easily lose you your job, but Colum was the head honcho at this particular office and he knew that Sharon had numerous reasons, fifty thousand to be precise, for not mounting a sexual harassment case against him.

'Oh, you are awful! But whilst I'm wearing this teeny-weeny miniskirt I don't think I dare.' Sharon stood up and twirled round as she spoke, revealing a black leather microskirt more appropriate for a King's Cross crack whore than the receptionist of a serious financial firm. Even Colum was slightly taken aback but, of course, he fully approved. 'But maybe one day you can take me for a ride.'

'You know, I might just do that . . . and maybe one day you can have a go on the back of my motorbike too!' Sharon had heard the depressingly obvious double entendre at least five times that year, but once again she tittered away as if in the presence of a comic genius. After a bit more playful banter Colum strutted towards his luxurious office. On the way he passed three of his junior partners, all of whom had arrived almost two hours before him. They were sitting in the open-plan part of the office and Colum was pleased to note the suitably deferential greetings that, as always, he received. He responded with a subtle nod of his head – a reminder, on the off chance that they needed one, of his superior status.

He closed his door, removed his £5,400 Gucci biker's jacket and took off his equally ludicrous leather trousers. Without bothering to cover his modesty with one of the pairs of chinos he kept in his office he fired up his computer and logged on to Reuters and Bloomberg – the two main news wires that delivered up-to-the-minute information about bonds, equities, commodities and corporate deals to financial whizzkids across the globe. He punched in Geldlust AG's codes and, sitting there in his white voluminous Y-fronts farting like a farmyard animal and wallowing in his own putrid stench, he contemplated the situation.

Geldlust was up another 2.3 per cent and six million shares had already been traded despite the market's having only been open twenty minutes. This was excellent news, and Colum smiled to himself. He looked at the related news-flow and discovered that at around 7 p.m. yesterday both Reuters and Bloomberg had noted Geldlust's share price appreciation and concluded that it was the result of takeover rumours. Outstanding. He picked up the newspapers that Sharon had, as usual, spread out in a crescent over his huge mahogany desk and scanned their financial sections. Both the *Telegraph*'s market report and that of the *Financial Times* mentioned Geldlust's share price rise and once again put it down to the possibility of an imminent acquisition by a 'large US bank with European ambitions'. The *Telegraph* quoted a representative of Geldlust giving the usual pat line that 'we never comment on market rumours' which, of course, was always liable to be interpreted as 'damn, you've hit the nail on the head'. Colum's face exploded into a maniacal grin and he began pounding his desk with his chubby fist. Nothing gave him greater pleasure than conning the market. He loved to tell any sucker dumb enough to listen the old poker adage that 'if you don't know who the fool around the table is . . . then it's you'. Colum took great pride in the fact that he was rarely, if ever, the fool.

He spent the next three hours calling up his favoured equity traders and stockbrokers across the City. He was a major client for all the bulge-bracket banks because he lobbed commission around like a demented coke slut chucking confetti at her best friend's wedding. Last year alone he had turned over his portfolio fifteen times which, given an average 0.2 per cent commission rate, meant that the banks he chose to deal with received over £30 million together. With hedge funds dropping like flies and commission hard to come by in a cautious post-credit crunch world it was no wonder those syphilitic cocksuckers treated him like a superstar. Now Colum was going to use the goodwill he had accrued over the previous decade to implement the most precisely coordinated one-man bear raid the world had ever witnessed.

He started by buying futures in Geldlust's equity. A futures contract obliges the owner to buy or sell an asset at a specific price on a specific date. They are theoretically used to hedge an investor's position in the underlying asset class but, in reality, are generally used by dodgy hedge funds to take highly geared bets that can easily garner ten times the return – or loss – that a conventional investment would yield.

Only the largest companies had futures contracts related to their share prices, and whilst Geldlust wasn't huge it used to be worth three times its market capitalisation before the credit crunch cut it down to size and it was a heavily traded stock; hence there were still futures in Geldlust. Colum used all his contacts to buy nine different futures contracts on Geldlust – the most highly geared ones money could buy. He bought €10 million worth granting him an obligation to sell stock in Geldlust in three, six and nine months' time at prices ranging from €42 to €51. He would have bought more but those trades had pretty much cleared out the books and were already moving the market. He quickly worked out that this investment alone would give him a profit of €230 million were Geldlust's share price to drop 38 per cent and reach €35, though he knew that such a drop was extremely optimistic.

He next bought €30 million of put options on Geldlust's equity. Unlike futures, these old-school derivatives gave him the right *but not the obligation* to sell Geldlust's shares at a certain price on *or before* a certain date. Again, they were a highly geared way of betting on a decline in Geldlust's share price. Then he got his sales trader to short as many Geldlust shares as possible. Within three hours Alpha Max had borrowed 1.5 per cent of the Geldlust equity, equating to 3.9 million shares worth €210 million, which it had then immediately sold on the market at an average price of €52. Already, despite the major buying by dumb schmucks who had fallen for the bullshit takeover story, Colum's aggressive trading was single-handedly pushing the Geldlust share price down dramatically.

There was only one trade left to do and it was the riskiest of the lot. Colum bought €35 million of Geldlust credit default swaps. These tricky little bad boys were not for the faint-hearted. They were supposed to be sold to pension funds and the like who had bought bonds from large corporations or, for that matter, countries. The CDSs were sold by banks as a form of insurance covering the interest payments that the corporation concerned was supposed to be paying out each year. If that company had a triple A credit rating you could buy them cheap as chips. If it then proved that the company could pay its creditors then they would be worth absolutely nothing, meaning Colum stood to potentially lose his whole €35 million wager. However, if concerns about the company's viability arose they'd suddenly rise dramatically in value. Geldlust's CDSs on 7 December were trading at €600,000 for every €100 million of debt insured. Colum did not expect Geldlust to go bust, but he knew that its CDSs could easily quadruple in value at the first sign of any major financial problems.

There was only one thing left to do before Colum could go off for his usual mid-afternoon rendezvous with one of the seven high class prostitutes he liked to visit to bring some colour to his working week. He called everyone he'd told the false Geldlust takeover story to and explained that he'd just spoken to someone very high up at the State of Saxony who had informed him that *Mein Kampf* would be a bestseller in Tel Aviv long before they sold off their controlling stake in Geldlust. He then called up his media contacts to 'educate' them about the 'ill-informed error' they had unfortunately made regarding Geldlust. A quick check half an hour later that Bloomberg had published the takeover-denial story and that Geldlust's share price was already starting a precipitous decline ensured that Colum could head out to see Simone safe in the knowledge that Operation Yogi was shaping up nicely. He put his trousers on, grabbed his jacket and took three ribbed 'big boy' condoms, a half-used tube of raspberry lube and two grams of Bolivia's finest out of his top drawer. He was already so excited about the day's work that he could have loaned out his schlong to De Beers for use as a diamond cutter. After he'd had his way, poor Simone would be walking like John Wayne for a month, he thought, licking his lips.

After a brief flirtation with Sharon he waltzed out looking fiendishly smug. Before he started up his bike he made one call, being sure to cover his offensively cheap mobile with his hand just in case one of his fellow hedgies walked by. He'd rather have been captured live on prime-time TV fucking a bearded camel than be seen in possession of such an outdated model. Rachel didn't answer so he left a short but eloquent message: 'Ring Piece, it's Cock Stick. Phase two of Yogi is complete. Time for your boys to step on Dog Shit.'

Then he started up his stallion and roared off to see the fourth most expensive prostitute in London.

Ten

Financial Services Authority
Tuesday, 7 December, 1.15 p.m. (€51.3, down
11.2% on the day)

'BUT JAMES, WITH ALL DUE respect, we simply cannot
afford to be caught napping again.'

Rachel had pulled out the big guns early on at
her meeting with her boss. All the members of Operation
Yogi had agreed in Cambridge that the most obvious way to
persuade the FSA to begin an investigation into Geldlust's
finances was to politely remind it of its dreadful performance
prior to the credit crunch. The FSA, together with the Bank
of England, was supposed to have made financial checks on
all banks with British operations to ensure that they were
financially viable. This was to nip in the bud any potential
contagion that could spread were one of them to go down.
Hence, the trillion-pound UK government bail-out
necessitated by the failure of banks like Northern Rock,

RBS and HBOS was a massive slap in the face for the City regulators who, as Colum had said during his presentation, had shamefully revealed themselves to be 'as useless as tits on a boar'.

Rachel had arranged this informal get-together in her boss's office immediately on hearing Colum's curt phone message and had spent the hours since preparing her spiel. But so far, much to her irritation, her boss wasn't biting. James Montague was a slimy scumbag who clearly felt he was too good for his job at the City regulator. Like most people in the FSA he envied the self-satisfied, highly paid arsewipes who worked in the City. He had seen three of his colleagues double their salaries over the previous year by taking senior positions in investment banks' compliance departments – which, in the current regulatory environment, were one of the few real growth areas in the Square Mile. Hardly a day went by when he didn't wonder why the call had never come for him, and the unthinkable possibility that it was due to his own failings gnawed away at his insides most nights.

Rachel didn't like the smarmy bell-end and her opinion of him hadn't improved after the married father of three had tried to get into her knickers after a few vodka and tonics at the local wine bar. As a mother who often felt more dowdy than sexy she might have been flattered had she not known he'd already tried it on with at least three other women in her department, one of whom made Susan Boyle look like Playmate of the Month. As she rebuffed his clumsy moves she remembered thinking that if this attempt at seduction was indicative of the FSA's competence then it was no wonder everyone in the City thought they were bungling twats. It pained her daily to be part of such a pointless organisation.

'Explain to me again exactly why we should investigate Geldlust.' There was a contrived weariness in James's nasal tones.

'OK . . . I met up with this source and she showed me some letters from Geldlust's CEO, Dr Herman Pfister, that are really worrying.' All the members of Yogi had agreed to refer to their 'source' at Geldlust as if she were a woman to throw people off the scent in case there ever was an investigation.

'And do you have any of these letters?' asked James, staring at the dirt under his fingernails. He was trying to picture what pants Rachel was wearing. If she had deigned to show him he would no doubt have been somewhat disappointed by the frayed, once-white M&S numbers that should have been thrown out years ago. His fetid imaginings featuring a hot pink dental floss thong were well wide of the mark.

'I have one letter, but there are several others and this is by far the least worrying. Unfortunately, my source took the others. She's scared and really doesn't want to lose her job just before bonuses are dolled out.' Rachel then showed the most damaging genuine letter that Steve had stolen. It spoke of off-balance-sheet SPVs and potentially higher costs related to the sub-prime mortgage situation than had been publicly revealed; but was probably not on its own sufficiently disturbing to warrant an investigation. Rachel had decided not to show her boss the doctored letters – partly because she wasn't comfortable doing something so criminal and partly because she believed the FSA wouldn't have had much truck with crude photocopies. Despite her misgivings about her job she wasn't going to jeopardise her only respite from the drudgery of a housewife's existence.

'OK . . . this is a little more interesting.' Rachel could see the rusty cogs in James's head spring into action. His eyes lit up as he imagined a successful early investigation of Geldlust proving to be a real feather in his cap. He was also uneasily aware of how bad he'd look if there were genuine issues and he was later shown to have passed up the opportunity to investigate the firm – something that little prick-tease Rachel would no doubt happily reveal to James's own boss were it to come to that. James had received a gentle slap on the wrist in early 2009 because he had rubber-stamped a report stating that Northern Rock was 'financially secure' just two months before it had endured the first run on a British bank for almost 150 years. He didn't want to be caught with his pants down again. 'I'll tell you what – you can head up a preliminary internal investigation to see if this is a case worth pursuing. I'll send an email round to see if any of the team have any useful insights. What you need to now do is: one, dig around some more for other evidence of a cover-up; two, get your source to give you all the documents she can get her hands on; and three, report back to me with your findings next Wednesday.'

Rachel got up to leave. She had no wish to spend any longer than necessary in James's oily presence.

After closing the door to her own office behind her she stood for a while with her eyes closed and her hands on her diaphragm, and breathing deeply from her stomach – using relaxation techniques her weekly yoga session had taught her. Suddenly she felt her lips curl into a sly smile. Much to her surprise, she realised that she was enjoying the buzz she was getting from her wrong-doing. Her life had been painfully bereft of joy for several years. It was so good to feel . . . alive. She let out a short laugh and then swiftly covered her mouth with her hand. Then she did it again. Within seconds she was chuckling away like a schoolgirl, tears of joy dripping down her cheeks as she half suppressed a full-scale attack of the giggles. Only after several minutes had she regained her composure sufficiently to call Fergus.

'Fuckwit, it's Ring Piece. Sorry to say this is not a total success . . . but we *are* beginning an unofficial, internal preliminary investigation into the affairs of Dog Shit plc. I'll bring over a hard copy of the email to your place this evening.'

Fergus said nothing.

The ball was now in his court.

Eleven

Steve's flat, Old Street
Wednesday, 8 December, 1.22 a.m.

I WAS LYING ON THE leather sofa in my sitting room, staring at the two empty bottles of Rioja standing on the coffee table, wondering if I'd ever get to sleep. I was wired and for once it wasn't the devil's dandruff that was to blame. I desperately wanted to kip but my mind was racing at a thousand miles an hour. I glanced at the near-empty wine glass in front of me and briefly contemplated retrieving another bottle from the rack . . . but I just couldn't be fucked to get up. Mr Tibbs casually strolled over. He looked as if he was about to jump on to me and I shooed him away. I wasn't in the mood and he had an evil look in his eye – there was simply no way I was going to let the little fucker anywhere near my plums.

I looked down at the clock on the DVD player again – 1.23 a.m. It was going to be all about Fergus in around twelve hours' time but the day after that I would come to the fore. Just thinking about what I was going to do made me feel nauseous. If I bottled it then Yogi was going to go off at half-cock. If I screwed up the rest of the team would never forgive me – especially Fergus. I had to be on the ball. I had to get some fucking sleep.

I tried to focus on our self-appointed mission. Fergus had been so militant about Yogi and we'd all become so caught up in his enthusiasm that we hadn't had time to think about the reality of what we were actually doing. At the 'off-site' in Cambridge it had almost seemed like a merry jape . . . a bit of fun for a bunch of friends. But as I lay there on my own contemplating our plan it didn't seem like fun any more. It was a major criminal enterprise – nothing more, nothing less. We had all tried to justify our participation in various disparate ways, but what we were doing was little different from putting stockings on our heads and brandishing a sawn-off at the local NatWest. We were stealing money, plain and simple, and no judge in the land would listen to our pathetic justifications; we would most certainly be going down for a long time should we get caught. I wondered if the others were thinking such dark thoughts. I suspected they were – especially Rachel, who had the most to lose. I shivered just thinking about what it would be like in the slammer. The very thought of it made me thirst after another drink.

I sat up, pulled the glass to my dry lips and downed the last of the Rioja. Bitter sediment stuck to my tongue and I spat it back into the glass. I closed my eyes momentarily but it was in vain; I realised that sleep was at best a few hours away. I felt the beginnings of a migraine coming on and massaged my temples hoping that it might make me feel better – it didn't. I resigned myself to another throbbing headache, reached for the remote control and turned on the vast plasma television that hung on the wall.

It was playing a repeat of a programme that I'd seen around this time last year, another one of those list shows that were constantly being broadcast in the absence of any original programming. This one was the top twenty financial bad boys of the naughties, and I sat back to watch a bunch of talking heads discuss the likes of Fred Goodwin, Jérôme Kerviel and Dick Fuld. I thought about whether any other decade would be able to parade such an impressive array of top class shysters and quickly concluded that we were in a golden age of financial wrong-doing. I wondered briefly whether any of our group might feature on a comparable list in nine years' time and prayed to God that we wouldn't.

It was whilst that rent-a-quote twat Cityboy was spouting off some bullshit about Bernie Madoff that the landline rang. I thought about blanking it but curiosity got the better of me. Generally, only my parents or one of the gang used my landline, and to call at this hour had to mean that something was up. I pulled myself to my feet, staggered to the desk and picked up the phone. 'Hello,' I croaked.

I was met with silence. I said 'hello' again but still received no response. After a few more seconds I said it a third time. I thought it must be a faulty line and told whoever it was to ring back.

I waited by the desk for thirty seconds but, on receiving no follow-up call, settled back on to the sofa. My eyelids began to grow heavy and for a brief moment it looked as though I might nod off, until I was suddenly snapped out of my fug by another sharp trill of the phone. This time I cursed whoever it was and leapt up angrily. I arrived at the desk and snatched the receiver to my ear. 'Hello,' I shouted with just enough aggression to let whoever was calling me know I was fucking irritated.

All I could hear now was the faint sound of breathing. 'Look, I can hear you. I know you're there,' I said. Nothing. 'Oh, for fuck's sake . . . if you think this is funny, grow up, OK?' I was just about to slam the receiver down when I heard a car horn sound in both ears. It came from outside the window and from the phone simultaneously.

I ran to the window, pulled the curtain to one side and, still holding the receiver to my ear, scanned the street outside. A lorry drove by, a young couple walked along chatting, but nothing else. I felt uneasy. This was beginning to give me the creeps.

I was about to head back to the sofa when suddenly I saw a puff of smoke and the glow of a cigarette in a shadowy doorway across the road. The brief illumination from the cigarette revealed the dim outline of a figure – someone in a hat and scarf. I felt my heartbeat quicken, and pushed my face so close to the window that my breath misted up the glass. I wiped away the condensation with my sleeve and stared at the doorway. Any feeling of tiredness had been replaced by heart-stopping fear. Who the fuck was outside? Why were they calling me? Was it someone who knew about our plans?

I pushed the receiver tight to my ear, held my breath and listened to my spy. There was nothing. Eventually I said: 'Listen, I can see you. Who the fuck is this? I'm gonna call the police.'

Again, I was greeted by silence . . . and then I heard a faint chuckle followed by a click. Whoever it was had hung up. I was left standing there in my boxer shorts staring at the shadows. After a few minutes I let the curtain fall back and dialled 1471, but of course the number was withheld.

I sat back down on the sofa, my mind racing. Someone was trying to scare me, but who? I could count on two hands the people who had my landline number. I'd not long moved flat and hadn't been able to bring my old telephone number with me. It was literally just my parents, the gang and the HR department at Geldlust who knew my digits. Why would any of them be trying to frighten me? What the fuck was going on?

After a nervous cigarette I went back to the window and pulled the curtains open an inch. I stared at the doorway opposite but it was now in total darkness. I stayed there for several minutes and saw nothing. Suddenly, a lorry drove by. It passed my flat and its headlights briefly lit up the doorway I was watching.

There was no one there.

I glanced up and down the street. There wasn't a soul out there.

I returned to my sofa. I was doing my best not to panic. I had another trembling cigarette. All I knew was that I didn't want to freak the others out. I wouldn't tell anyone in the gang about this.

I put the TV back on and settled down to another sleepless night.

Twelve

The White Hart pub, Clifton Street
Wednesday, 8 December, 1.35 p.m.
(€49.4, down 3.3% on the day)

FERGUS STUMBLED BACK FROM THE crowded bar bearing a tray with five pints of Continental lager and a double whisky. He shakily handed out the beers to his associates and placed one of the pints and the whisky in front of himself. After falling into his seat he somewhat theatrically downed the whisky and then took a huge gulp of his beer. He wiped the froth from his mouth with his forearm and grinned like a village idiot.

One of the other journalists round the table, a despicable, treacherous midget called Reynolds, took a measured sip of his own pint and then exclaimed in his irritating cockney drawl, 'You're not fucking around today, mate, are you? Trying to remember something or trying to forget something?'

Even before he'd finished his sentence, Reynolds realised his mistake. There was a sharp intake of breath from the others at the table and Reynolds was suddenly gripped by a fascination with his shoes. Only two of the lads had ever met Bridget but they were all aware of her recent death. After an awkward pause Fergus broke the silence.

'Nah . . . I'm celebrating,' he slurred.

Another journo, Thomas, desperately relieved that the conversation had not veered on to Fergus's girlfriend's suicide, piped up: 'Oh yeah? What are you celebrating? The *Guardian* haven't given you another hundred and fifty quid a year raise, have they?' There were a few drunken titters from the assembled hacks.

'I'm celebrating something . . . well, I shouldn't really tell you this, but . . . fuck it! I've uncovered something pretty big and I reckon after my story goes out tomorrow it's going to be front page news across the world.' He grinned in as self-satisfied manner as he could muster.

Fergus had assembled four fellow journalists for his piss-up – a motley crew of wild-eyed lash-heads and feckless onanists, notorious even within their own sleazy trade for having the moral capacity of hammerhead sharks and the unrestrained bestial urges of rabid baboons. Reynolds worked at Thomson Reuters covering the banks sector and Thomas, a porcine sot and notorious sodomite, worked at Bloomberg. The other two – Robert, a vicious pervert and remorseless dope-fiend, and Huw, a revolting pus-faced sleazemonger who allegedly tortured kittens for kicks – worked for the *FT* and the *Telegraph* respectively. They had all known each other for years but they were by no means the best of friends. In reality, they were competitors who phoned each other now and again to boast about how well they were doing or sneakily garner some information for a story. They were all in the mid-thirties and had at one time or another worked with each other.

Fergus had called them on Tuesday to arrange today's liquid lunch, saying that it would be nice to 'see the lads and sink a few like we did in the old days'. They normally wouldn't have bothered turning up but they were all aware of Fergus's recent tragedy and even such morally bankrupt piranhas felt that to avoid this particular session would have been bad form. In any case, they hardly needed an excuse to knock back a few.

They had assumed that Fergus was desperately lonely and that the drink would be a mournful, sombre affair, but within minutes of arriving they had settled into their favourite pastime: bitching and gossiping about other journalists. Apart from Reynolds, who wasn't the sharpest tool in the pack, they had all noticed Fergus's rapid drinking and concluded that he had turned to alcohol for solace following his recent loss. What none of them realised was that every time Fergus bought a round he ordered an alcohol-free lager for himself, and that whenever he went to the gents he took any pint that had been bought for him and poured half of it away. He was, in fact, the soberest hack round the table . . . and, for that matter, probably the soberest hack in London on that cold and breezy Wednesday afternoon.

'Oh, really? I don't suppose you'd be so kind as to divulge to your old pals here what the great Fergus Callahan, "the scourge of City malpractice and defender of the little people", is about to reveal to the world? Are those horrid, nasty bankers going to award themselves big bonuses again? Or has another Wall Street cad conned a few more Florida pensioners?' A few half-hearted snorts of laughter greeted Rob's caustic sarcasm. Fergus's drinking partners were bonded by a kind of journalistic inverse snobbery – a contempt for any of their kind who were foolish enough to think they were doing the world some good.

'Well . . . if you really want to know . . . some documents have come into my hands that show that a certain large German bank is in deep shit and has not revealed its status to either the German or the British regulators. The FSA are so worried they've ordered an investigation. This fucker could go bust! This could be the start of credit crunch mark two!' Fergus babbled. 'Look . . . I'll show you a few of the docs but don't go blathering to other people about it, at least not until tomorrow.'

Suddenly Fergus had a completely rapt audience. They were all stunned that he was revealing his exclusive, something no right-thinking journalist would ever do, and could only conclude that his drunkenness and recent tragedy were resulting in a serious bout of unprofessionalism. And of course, being the savage pimps they were, they were only too happy to exploit their bereaved colleague's apparent inebriation for their own sick ends – just as Fergus had known they would be.

Fergus held up a few of the doctored letters and the FSA email Rachel had given him the night before. He folded them clumsily, pretending that he was trying to hide the name of the bank involved, but only a half-blind smack-head would not have seen the Geldlust Bank headed paper. He read out a few choice morsels, being sure to slur each word longer than two syllables, and drunkenly pushed back the eager hands that tried to grab the letters off him. The half-cut degenerates at his table had all sobered up extremely quickly. They knew what Fergus was showing them was 100 per cent pure gold. When they realised that they weren't going to be able to snatch the rest of the documents off Fergus – whose reactions seemed remarkably sharp considering his debilitated state – they quickly manufactured excuses as to why they suddenly had to head back to their offices. Within about nine minutes Fergus was sitting alone surrounded only by half-emptied pint glasses and the rancid stench of cynical treachery.

He wasn't surprised by their actions. Recent events had further deepened his already profound mistrust of human nature and these hacks really were the lowest of the low. He briefly wondered whether journalists were an even more despicable breed than bankers and quickly concluded that it was too close to call. He started mentally listing the professions that had proved to be populated by dishonest shysters over recent years. He thought of MPs and policemen, Catholic priests and lawyers. It seemed as if there was no one out there who wasn't playing for the devil's team . . . no one perhaps apart from him.

After a suitable wait he stood up and walked straight to the exit with a strong and steady step. Considering his slobbering drunkenness of just a few minutes before, those of his fellow lunchtime drinkers who saw his remarkable transformation would later swear that they had witnessed a miracle unseen since Lazarus rose from the dead.

Fergus was back at the *Guardian* office in Islington within half an hour of boarding the tube at Liverpool Street station. He had a short coffee break and then went to check out one of only three Bloomberg machines owned by his penny-pinching employer. He smiled with grim satisfaction when he saw that Thomas had already published an online story about Geldlust. Thomas's short article had gone out at 3.05 p.m. and he had written it cleverly; it was sufficiently vague to be legally watertight but comprehensive enough to leave the reader in no doubt that Thomas knew all the details and, most important, that he was the first journalist to reveal them.

16 December, 3.05 p.m.
Breaking News/Exclusive
Major regulatory concerns about Geldlust's financial disclosure
By Thomas Liddell

Bloomberg has learnt that the Financial Services Authority (the FSA) is conducting an investigation into the financial viability of the large German bank, Geldlust (GDL AG, market capitalization €11.9bn).

There is speculation that Geldlust has used off-balance-sheet special purpose vehicles to hide its continuing exposure to the US sub-prime mortgage market and that it also has major liabilities associated with derivatives – namely credit default swaps (CDSs).

The FSA and Geldlust have been contacted but neither has been willing to comment though neither has denied that the investigation is taking place.

Geldlust's share price has been falling over recent days and is down 5.4% today at €48.3.

Perfect, thought Fergus. It was now 3.15 p.m. and the story had been out for ten minutes. It was time to see what impact the Bloomberg story had made. The market usually responded extremely quickly to dramatic announcements like this one – especially when there was not much more than an hour of trading left. Still, when Fergus typed in Geldlust's Bloomberg code he could hardly believe what he saw. He clenched his right hand into a fist and punched the palm of left hand triumphantly, his eyes wide open with shock and glee. He hadn't felt so excited for months – this was going far better than he had thought possible. Geldlust's share price was already down another 15 per cent and trading had been temporarily suspended, in the hope that rationality would replace panic in an hour or so – there was blood on the streets.

By the end of the trading day Geldlust's share price stood at €39.5, down 23 per cent. Pleasingly, Reynolds's article that came out on Reuters at 3.25 p.m. had seemed to confirm Bloomberg's story to the market. Combined with the downward price pressure resulting from Provincial Mutual's offloading of stock and Alpha Max's short-selling, the rumour was creating a vicious circle that was decimating Geldlust's share price. Fergus knew that the stock market hates uncertainty more than anything else, and that when there is a range of possible outcomes the market tends to factor in the worst-case scenario until proved wrong. Heated conversations between sweaty stockbrokers on trading floors across the City were undoubtedly already mentioning names like Enron, Lehmans and RBS.

At precisely 4.30 p.m., at the close of the German and UK stock markets, Fergus approached his boss, Bob Beamon, the overall editor of the *Guardian*'s financial section. Bob was considered to be just another harmless dipsomaniac by his fellow hacks and his lonely, sordid trips to Bangkok and Phnom Penh were the stuff of Fleet Street legend. Fergus knew that the dramatic Geldlust share price fall combined with his highly respected investigative reputation would make Bob's agreement to put his Geldlust article on the front page of the finance section a mere formality. He had, of course, already written it and it was a work of pure genius.

He had spent a sleepless night employing all his literary skills to make Geldlust's woes sound incredibly worrying without saying anything that could be denied outright or deemed libellous. All the claims he made were based on half-truths, meaning that any denials would have to be qualified which would make them significantly less reassuring. He confirmed that the FSA were conducting an investigation into Geldlust's financial situation without mentioning that it was merely an informal and preliminary one. The beauty of his lunchtime meeting with his so-called friends was that his own Geldlust article would now appear alongside many others in Thursday's press, thereby granting credibility to the story and meaning Fergus would be less likely to be singled out were there to be a regulatory investigation. However, his article would be far more detailed than those of his peer group and would have by far the biggest share price impact. He knew that it would be the main source of information for the lazy me-too journalists of the weekend press, who would all go mad over this story as they strived to make sure they didn't miss a potential upcoming disaster – another unforeseen consequence of the credit crunch that so many had hoped was over.

Fergus handed in his story to his boss at 7.25 p.m. Bob was sitting in his office alone drinking a quarter pint of cheap whisky out of a stained coffee mug in the vague hope that his colleagues wouldn't notice. He scanned the article and, once Fergus had agreed that he would stand up in court to defend his story if necessary, confirmed that it would be on the business section's front page.

At 7.45 p.m. Fergus was walking out of the *Guardian*'s front door with a spring in his step and a grin on his face.

It looked as though nothing could go wrong.

Thirteen

Geldlust trading floor
Thursday, 9 December, 8.45 a.m.
(€32.7, down 17.2% on the day)

GELDLUST'S TRADING FLOOR WAS IN complete turmoil. Unrestrained panic was in the air. There'd been nothing like this since the fall of Lehmans in September '08. Each fall in Geldlust's share price seemed to notch up the tension for the salesmen and traders who were anxiously watching their personal wealth decline at a frightening pace. Some of the juniors were running around like headless chickens whilst the elder traders were presenting an image of contrived nonchalance that was fooling no one. Everyone was shouting down their phones and there was only one subject being discussed. Clients from across the world who owned shares in Geldlust wanted to know the inside story and were calling up any contacts they had at the bank. Shareholders were panicking and dumping their stock – especially those speculative buffoons who had foolishly bought the shares as a result of the takeover rumours Colum had spread. The impact of the morning's press articles had been brutal and the acrid stench of sweaty fear was everywhere.

As usual, the measured German management team had not made any formal comment. Their MO was to never comment on market rumours, and they were unsure how to react. Everything was happening so fast. The CEO, Dr Pfister, happened to be on a flight to Japan, which made his subordinates all the more confused about what they should do. They were like rabbits in the headlights and their inaction was scaring everybody. That the banking equity analyst at Geldlust was not allowed to make formal recommendations regarding his own bank added to the confusion. He had made a few brief remarks at the 7.20 a.m. morning meeting but they were vague and based on mere speculation. However, Chris Browning had, somewhat unusually, made a final comment after the formal part of the morning meeting was over. He had done his best to reassure everyone by spouting off meaningless terms like 'financially viable for the foreseeable future' and he had told everyone on the trading floor to call up Geldlust's shareholders and instil some confidence in them. This uncoordinated strategy was likely to prove completely counter-productive because any institutional investor who received five or so garbled and possibly contradictory messages from disparate Geldlust employees would undoubtedly conclude that we really were in trouble . . . that 'the lady doth protest too much'.

I sat there watching the panic-stricken hordes feeling a grim satisfaction in our work. I was still feeling jittery about my early morning visitor two nights before but dismissed my fears – there was work to be done. I took out the list of Geldlust's top one hundred shareholders that I'd composed three days before and began ringing them all up. Nearly all were on answerphone and it only took me two hours to leave a short, superficially reassuring message for each of them. It went something like this: 'Hi, Gunter, I just wanted to call you re this Geldlust situation. I don't think there's anything to worry about . . . really. Our shareholder reserves stand at ten billion euros and we said at our half-year results that we were on course to make a three per cent return on equity this year. As regards this talk of SPVs and so forth . . . well, erm, we don't really know about those but I'm sure it's all fine . . . probably.'

I had purposely made the calls unpersuasive, and had used my trading desk phone knowing that the recordings might prove vital for my defence were there an investigation at a later date. I needed evidence that suggested I had done my best to reassure all concerned parties. I had also made the calls loudly enough for all my colleagues who were within earshot to have no doubt as to where my loyalties lay. However, as soon as I had finished leaving those messages I sloped off into a private unused office and turned on a third mobile phone that I'd been given by Fergus for just this occasion. Then I took out a different list of Geldlust's top shareholders. It had taken me several hours to compile this one, mainly using our firm's client database but also by speaking to my fellow traders and salesmen. It contained the mobile phone numbers of those on my previous list whom I'd actually met . . . excluding the Obergruppenführers at the State of Saxony who were obviously never going to sell. I started calling those on the list to deliver a starkly different message from the one I'd been publicly broadcasting. This time, if they didn't answer, I hung up. There was no question of leaving any proof of my malicious intent. The new conversations went something like this:

Me: Hi, Matthias, it's Steve at Geldlust.

Matthias: Hello, Steve.

Me: Now listen, Matthias, I know I left a brief voicemail with you this morning, but I wanted to give you the real deal about Geldlust . . . I'm only doing this because we know each other and you've been a good client . . . and I really don't want to bullshit you with the official line. I'm taking a big risk doing this so mum's the word where you heard this from, OK?

Matthias: Erm . . . Vat must I do with your mum?

Me: Sorry, I just mean that you mustn't tell anyone who told you this information, OK?

Matthias: Ja, OK.

Me: Look, I'm afraid I don't think the situation here is very good at all. The MDs are rushing around like headless chickens and I'm hearing from some serious dudes here that we have some *major* liabilities which will be revealed at the trading statement on the seventeenth if not before. The market is going to crucify this company and, despite the recent share price decline, I would seriously get the *hell* out of Geldlust stock ASA fucking P. We could have another Lehmans here . . .

Matthias: Scheisse.

After an hour of these calls I went back to the trading floor and discovered a hellish atmosphere of bewilderment, depression and abject horror. The volume on the screens that hung from the ceiling had been turned up and many of my colleagues were simply staring at them in utter disbelief. CNBC and Bloomberg Television were focusing on one story and one story only. There was even talk from some commentators that Geldlust's woes could pull down other banks with it – exactly the same concerns that were voiced in September 2008 after the fall of Lehmans. The market was down 4.5% and the whole financial sector was taking a savage beating. Some of the other German banks like Deutsche and Commerzbank were already down 9 to 12 per cent. One gormless economic analyst, whom they always wheeled out in these situations, said that we faced another possible credit crunch. He claimed that his sources at other banks were already saying they were contemplating ceasing all trading with Geldlust until the 'situation' was cleared up. They didn't want to face exposing themselves to a sinking ship that could take them down with it. People were huddled around the screens looking like French aristocrats awaiting the guillotine. It felt as if World War Three had just broken out. As soon as I got to my desk I checked the Geldlust share price. I couldn't believe what I saw.

Geldlust AG, €25.2 (down 36.2 per cent), 24 million shares traded, temporarily suspended.

Christ alive, we had reached 'total capitulation' – the market had made its mind up that Geldlust was going to be the next Lehmans and every prick in town was selling. Even the bulls who had previously viewed the weakness as a buying opportunity had thrown in the towel. Simply no one was buying and the share price was in free fall. Our project was now going too well for my liking. I even heard some of my fellow salesmen advising people to dump their Geldlust stock, which seemed incomprehensible. The rumours of imminent bankruptcy that were swirling around seemed to be confirmed by the share price decline, which in turn had led to more selling and further share price depression and so on. It was almost too painful to watch. I was sweating like a rapist and my hands were shaking. I tiptoed around my colleagues feeling like a Judas who had secretly condemned them all to crucifixion.

Suddenly a red-faced, panting Chris Browning rushed out of his corridor to the mike, barging dumbfounded spectators out of the way as he did so. He struggled with the controls for a few seconds and then spoke. Everyone shut up and listened intently. Even those on the phone to clients ceased talking so they could hear whether the firm they worked for was about to go belly up. A once noisy, bustling room became eerily quiet.

'OK, everyone . . . erm . . . look, I know this looks really worrying . . . but please, please don't . . . erm, worry, that is.' His voice was shaking with emotion. He looked like a broken man. I'd never seen him in such a state and it certainly did not inspire confidence. He continued: 'I've just come off the phone with Dr Pfister and there will be an internal email sent round within an hour or so, followed by a press release. We are literally just dotting the i's and crossing the t's as we speak. As you know, I am not at liberty to disclose what this price-sensitive statement will say . . . but . . . let's just say I think you'll be quite pleased. That's it.' Chris had taken a risk even hinting that the management statements would be received positively. Compliance were almost certainly getting their soiled knickers in a twist about his chosen words but these were desperate times and they required desperate measures. He left the podium and received a few half-hearted cheers as he rushed back to his office.

I took stock of the situation. Geldlust shares were now down 55 per cent since we'd started our bear raid. Make no mistake, we had the critters by the short and curlies. Unless something extremely unusual happened we were all going to be multi-millionaires. After approximately three seconds of judicious consideration I decided it was time to crystallise our gains. I went back to the empty office

I'd used before and called up Fergus on my Brick Lane mobile.

'Fuckwit, it's Skidders. Listen, I think we should stop now. Let's close all our positions. This has gone too *fucking* well! Let's cash in our chips, mate, while we can. They're putting out an internal statement in about an hour and a press release after that. Surely there's no way the shares are going lower than this?' I desperately wanted him to say yes. There was no need to take this further. Any joy that I felt about my imminent enrichment was tempered by the pain I was causing my colleagues – quite a few of whom were half-decent folk. What had seemed like a giggle at first was proving to be a vicious attack that was going to hurt a lot of people. When I heard Fergus's response my shoulders dropped.

'No dice, Skid Mark. I've just called Cock Stick and we agree that if we implement phase four we can take Dog Shit plc down further. You've got the memory stick, yeah?'

'Yeah . . . I have,' I sighed. I hoped that my voice betrayed my distinct lack of enthusiasm. I really didn't want to implement phase four. We, or more specifically I, would now be taking the criminal behaviour up a notch. 'Look, Fuckwit, I don't know if we should do this . . . we've won already; can't we just call it a day?'

'No . . . we're taking those suckers down. This is for Bridget, remember? Do your *fucking* job like we all agreed.' His steely voice gave me no option. It was the brusque, intimidating tone of a man who wouldn't take no for an answer.

'OK . . . OK . . . I'll fucking do it,' I hissed through gritted teeth.

'Good. Don't fuck this up.'

I terminated the conversation and stared at the mobile for a minute. My heart was pumping away. I steadied myself and looked at my watch. It was 1.30 p.m. – three more hours of trading. I pulled out the memory stick Fergus's IT genius mate had given him and put it into the computer in the corner of the room. I booted the machine up, double-clicked on the skull and crossbones icon that popped up and downloaded a virus that was apparently so brutal that Geldlust's entire system, in London, Frankfurt, New York, Milan and Madrid, would be disabled within fifteen minutes. The Geldlust firewall would almost certainly have prevented anyone from infecting our network from the outside, but like most banks Geldlust wasn't prepared for a sophisticated virus spread from within by a treacherous bastard who wanted his own company to fail. I had been reassured that there was no way that this virus could be traced or that anyone would be able to discern that it had been an inside job. Within minutes the computer's screen went blank and then torrents of green numbers began filling the screen. It was as though the matrix had been revealed . . . and I was starting to panic.

As I pulled the memory chip out I sent a short prayer to the great Regulator in the sky. I had no doubt that if I was caught doing this I'd be facing a long stretch in prison. I walked as calmly as I could back to the trading floor to be greeted by complete pandemonium. Disbelief and horror had been replaced by blind panic. All the screens in the room were displaying the same hypnotic green numbers scrolling down the screen. Some people were shouting whilst others held their heads in their hands. I saw Chris Browning standing by the coffee machine watching the madness. He was as white as a sheet and looked close to tears. I surmised that there would be no reassuring press release for the next twenty-four hours at least. We really were through the looking glass now.

The next two hours were excruciating. IT guys rushed around completely out of their depth and unable to offer any help. It was quite clear that their usual advice to turn your machine off and on simply wasn't going to cut the mustard this time. Whilst some salesmen and traders were working their phones, others huddled in groups and muttered conspiratorially. I walked around racked with guilt, pretending to be as worried as everyone else and listened in to their conversations. Much to my surprise many of those on the phone weren't trying to reassure their clients; rather they were calling up headhunters and their pals at other banks and asking if there were any vacancies. Those who were standing around in groups weren't discussing whether to pile into Geldlust stock but were instead trying to ascertain which other firms might be taking on staff. The whole atmosphere was completely surreal. Analysts, corporate financiers and the back office boys had wandered on to the trading floor and stood staring at the post-apocalyptic hell that greeted them. Nearly everyone in sight had some kind of handheld device out, be it an iPhone or a BlackBerry, and was using it to keep track of the news-flow and the ever-decreasing Geldlust share price. Big Al, not a man known for his subtlety or his consideration for the feelings of others, would shout out the price every time it dropped a euro. In the space of twenty minutes I heard his gruff Essex drawl shout down from 22 euros to 20. The effect on team morale was predictable. Another character sitting at the far end of the trading floor was adding to the mayhem by calling out major bits of related news-flow. Every ten or so minutes his more refined tones would ring out, delivering ever more depressing pieces of information that were greeted by a collective groan from the assembled hordes.

'HSBC says it's suspended trading with Geldlust "until the situation has been clarified".'

'Respected Wall Street analyst claims that a continued loss of market confidence could have a negative impact on sovereign debt in Greece, Portugal and Ireland.'

'German stock market suspends trading in Geldlust shares for an hour, again.'

'FSA confirms that it has launched an investigation into Geldlust,' and so forth.

I sat back down at my desk and logged in to Reuters on the iPad that I had bought for the occasion. That last message of doom from the thoughtful chap on the far side of the trading floor had confirmed that Rachel had done her job. A concise press release from the regulator confirming that an investigation was taking place had finally been issued. Pleasingly, it made no mention of the fact that it was internal or preliminary. I suspected that Rachel's boss, a prime pork penis by all accounts, wanted to appear ahead of the curve should things start getting serious. He was simply covering his back the way every motherfucker in the City had been taught to do from day one.

I used my iPad to log in to several oft-used unofficial financial websites that Fergus had been feeding information to. He was able to do this anonymously and these websites were, for reasons I'd never fully comprehended, enormously influential in the City. I nodded with grim satisfaction as I read through several of his articles. There were three main elements that had his signature all over them. First were charts comparing Geldlust's recent share price decline with those of Lehmans, Bear Stearns and RBS just before they got into real trouble. There appeared to be a remarkable similarity between them, but I knew that Fergus had simply adjusted the time line and scale to make them appear comparable. Second were excerpts from the press releases that firms like Enron, RBS and Worldcom had issued just prior to collapsing. The one from Lehmans of 10 September 2008, five days before it went bust, was particularly comical. It included the phrase 'the firm remains committed to examining all strategic alternatives to maximising strategic value' and claimed that stockholders' equity stood at $28.4 billion. Any press release Geldlust finally issued was now more likely to be seen as just another example of a doomed company desperately spin-doctoring to save its sorry arse. Finally, Fergus had uploaded some carefully selected scans of the same doctored letters that had conned his group of degenerate hacks into writing their damaging articles. The scans that Fergus had provided were at an angle as if they had been hastily placed on a photocopying machine and none of them showed any dates or who the letters were addressed to or from. This ensured that they could not be easily dismissed as fraudulent by Geldlust's executives until they had guaranteed that no one within the management team had written them, which could further delay their press release. Fergus, the sick bastard, knew that confirmation that the documents were not genuine could take many hours.

It was whilst I was staring at my iPad that I sensed a presence behind me. I felt a musty aura sweep across to my side of the trading floor long before its physical manifestation appeared. There was no doubt that some evil being was standing directly behind me. My stomach turned to water. I froze in my seat. My nose twitched. I had never experienced such a horrible sensation before. I slowly gathered the courage to turn round and see what dark phantom had come to haunt me; as I did so I felt my heart rate rise and a film of cold sweat dampen my forehead.

It was Richard Stimp and he needed to start using a deodorant ASAP.

He was looking over my shoulder at the iPad that I'd

placed on my desk. He had an angry scowl on his face. I needed to keep my cool and not overplay my hand.

'Fucking hell, you gave me a shock there, Richard! This is awful, just awful, isn't it?' I was desperately trying to imagine what a normal Geldlust employee would say in this situation.

There was a long, worrying pause. Suspicion was etched deep into his rat-like countenance. 'Hmm. It would have been a lot more awful for you had you not just sold all your shares. You know, some of us in Compliance think this is nothing more than an extremely sophisticated bear raid. I couldn't help but notice that your pal Fergus wrote one of the articles this morning damning Geldlust. I think you fuckers are up to something. You'd better not be, because I've got my eye on you and your pathetic group of friends.' My heart sank. This was unexpected. I had to style this out using all my finely honed bullshitting skills. I recalled Grouch Marx's classic idiom, 'If you can fake sincerity you've got it made', and decided that 'genuine' outrage and indignation seemed the appropriate reactions.

'You must be *fucking* mad! I had over two hundred grand in Geldlust stock that's now worth a third of what it was two weeks ago. You'd better not say anything to anyone else about your schoolboy suspicions or I will *fucking* sue you for libel, you snidey little *wanker*. Don't let your jealousy get the better of you, *dick splash*. Now get the fuck out of here before I get really angry.'

Richard's face turned bright pink. He looked as though he would like to stab me in the eye with the biro that peaked out of his shirt pocket. I realised that I might have slightly overdone it and, annoyingly, my outraged stream of invective had succeeded in causing a lot of heads to crane in my direction. A public airing of Richard's suspicions was the last thing I needed, but after a few seconds Richard regained his composure and turned to leave. Just before he did so he stuttered: 'Well, I . . . I hope for your sake that this has nothing to do with you, because believe me, if it has we *will* find out about it.'

As he scuttled off back to the lifts I turned round to my neighbours and shrugged my shoulders and lifted my hands in complete disbelief. All eyes were on me. If ever a De Niro tour de force was needed it was now.

'What the fuck? All that wanking over internet porn has turned that slimy cock jockey's brain to mush!' There were a few muffled laughs and much to my relief everyone turned round to talk amongst themselves again.

I felt uneasy. I sat there staring into the middle distance, my right leg jigging up and down on the floor like a pneumatic drill. I began to wonder if we'd been stupid. Could Richard put all the pieces of the jigsaw together and realise that a cabal of his old university foes had been instrumental in destroying his bank? I went through all the evidence. On paper it did look pretty damn suspicious but it seemed impossible to prove any wrong-doing. All our phone calls had been made using untraceable mobiles. No one at John's firm, whose selling had begun the panic, would admit to being duped because that would show that they had been willing to use inside information. No, Provincial Mutual would simply claim to be lucky or smart, as would Colum's outfit. None of the journalists who'd published damaging stories would admit to hearing the rumours about Geldlust from Fergus, and his article was just one of many that came out this morning. The letter Rachel had used to persuade the FSA that Geldlust was in trouble was a legitimate one and the additional information that had so helpfully appeared on the financial websites had been provided anonymously. No one would ever know that I had started the computer virus. I smiled to myself as I realised that even if Richard worked out that it was probably us who had brought his bank to its knees he was really going to struggle to prove it. I let out a snort of derision as I pictured the little tosspot's frustration as he came to realise that we were the culprits but found himself unable to do anything about it.

Suddenly I heard another disheartening groan of horror spread across the trading floor. I looked at my iPad. Big red headlines shouted out that the German Stock Exchange had suspended trading in Geldlust shares again. It had the right to cease all trading after a 10 per cent fall and Geldlust had dropped over twice that since the last suspension. It was the sheer speed of the share price decline that had allowed it to fall so far. The Reuters story suggested trading would recommence tomorrow. Share suspensions like this were often followed by another huge drop in price once trading restarted, as they tended to stoke the fires of panic whilst also creating a road block for sellers that once unplugged could lead to a massive outflow of stock on to the market without buyers to soak it up. However, if the Geldlust management could get their shit together and issue a really reassuring press release they might just be able pull the share price back up. Our gang had to simply hope that their shockingly incompetent behaviour continued.

I looked at my watch. It was 4.15 p.m. The market would close in fifteen minutes and Geldlust's share price stood at €18.5, down 53% on the day. Amazingly, there was still no statement from Geldlust. The virus had obviously prevented the required managers from signing off on the press release; I suspected that the execs were being typically German and had forfeited a rapid response to Geldlust's woes in favour of making sure their message was valid and legally water-tight. None of them wanted to reassure the market if there really were problems, as the leaked doctored letters seemed to suggest. If they did that they could find themselves criminally liable and land themselves in the same kind of trouble as execs at other distressed firms that had reassured the market just before their companies went bust: ending up in prison for market manipulation. MDs may be keen to save the firm they work for and understandably desperate to keep their stock options above water, but the threat of a spell in prison had shown itself once again to be a very effective incentive to err on the side of caution when issuing public statements.

Some of the lads were going to the boozer and I was

invited to join them by Big Al. While the prospect of sitting around with a bunch of depressed bankers chatting morbidly about their upcoming struggle to pay Tarquin's Harrow fees was appealing, I politely declined. Instead, I wandered home in a daze, my evil deeds clawing away at my conscience. I'd go back and chill out with Mr Tibbs. At least I had nothing to feel guilty about as far as that little fucker was concerned, through admittedly my gonads would have been considerably safer in the Red Lion.

Fourteen

Geldlust trading floor
Friday, 10 December, 6.55 a.m. (€18.5)

THE ATMOSPHERE ON THE TRADING floor was like nothing I'd ever experienced before. Usually there would be a hum and a buzz – the noise of excited chatter and of money being conjured out of thin air. Frantic panic and bewildered disbelief had been ruling the roost yesterday but this morning was different. Few people were speaking and when they did it was in hushed tones. There was no banter, no orders being shouted across the floor and no raucous laughter from the traders. The silence was unnatural and unnerving. The IT experts had been struggling with the computer virus all night and had still not got the systems functioning at full capacity. Some computers were working whilst others stared blankly back at us. Assorted rumours had been passing to and fro amongst the sales force but one thing was certain: there would be a stock market announcement from Geldlust's CEO at 7 a.m. Big bad Dr Pfister was finally going to sock it to us. People crowded around the monitors that were suspended from the ceiling every thirty feet or so. It felt like a bookie's minutes before the finish of the Grand National but this time it was our careers at stake. I looked around at the ashen faces of my colleagues, desperately trying to rid myself of the feelings of guilt and remorse. I had caused this distress. I was the reason why their company faced possible annihilation. Some of these guys had been working at Geldlust for over twenty years and they were going to struggle to find a job elsewhere. Their whole world was crashing down around them and it was because of me and my friends. Everyone was putting on a brave face but the tension was palpable. Even Big Al looked concerned.

We waited, and we waited some more.

The regulatory news service announcements began popping up on the working screens at precisely 7 a.m. The headlines in red first and then the detailed reports. First came a risible pre-closed season trading statement from the Royal Bank of Scotland, then some debilitatingly dull interim regulatory report from the Italian electricity regulator. Suddenly, the Geldlust statement flashed up. After a collective intake of breath someone whose computer was fully functioning pulled it up, clicked on it and began reading it aloud. About thirty of us gathered around his desk and I saw that similar groups had formed around the other desks lucky enough to have working computers. After the usual formalities and caveats the statement concluded: '. . . and the board of Geldlust will make a further announcement at 12 o'clock GMT today to clarify the situation. We have been informed by BaFin, the German financial regulator, that shares in Geldlust will not be suspended up until then.'

That was it. This time there was a collective sigh of disappointment. Another five hours of confusion and uncertainty stretched before us. People began chatting to each other in more animated tones as we slowly filed back to our desks. There was only one subject of conversation: was Geldlust going bust or not. There had been a lot of speculation from financial experts and politicians alike on television the previous night and opinion was split fairly evenly. I had watched respected financial journalists query whether this was the tail end of the credit crunch coming back to bite us on the arse. European stock markets had fallen 6 per cent on Thursday as the panic had begun to spread to other sectors and the Cassandras were shouting from the rooftops that we were in the middle of a 'major correction' – in other words a market decline of at least 20 per cent. This morning's headline on the front page of the *Sun* was simply CRASH! and one of the sub-headings read 'Just when you thought it was safe to re-enter the stock market . . .' over a picture of a shark with Pfister's head superimposed on to it. I couldn't believe how serious things had become. I began to think about the collapse of Lehmans back in September 2008. Had there been a conspiratorial group experiencing the same mixed emotions I was feeling as they saw the global economy grind to a halt as a result of their actions? Were we, like them, the straw that broke the camel's back?

At 8 a.m. stock markets across Europe opened. All eyes watched the fate of one company and one company only. It felt as if the fate of the world was in the balance and that we were in the eye of the storm. The grey market in Geldlust shares had suggested they would fall slightly but then something happened that no one expected. Geldlust shares began to edge up. There were a few muted, semi-ironic cheers but no one seriously believed that we were out of the woods just yet. I heard colleagues on the phone talking about 'bottom fishing' and others dismissing the 7 per cent share price rise as a 'dead cat bounce'. The price hovered around €19 for most of the early morning but the volumes were impressively high. Someone, somewhere had the balls to be trading this stock when it would be clear in a few hours whether it was dead meat or not. Stock markets in Frankfurt, Milan, Madrid and London responded with a 1 to 2 per cent rise so the champagne corks weren't being popped just yet.

I looked at the bottom right hand corner of my computer screen – 11.15 a.m. A few tense, unproductive hours had slipped by. I stared into nothingness. Suddenly, I felt the mobile in my pocket vibrate. It was the left pocket – the one with the brick in it. I pulled it out. It was Cock Stick. I looked around furtively, lowered my head and answered it in a conspiratorial whisper.

'Skid Mark, it's Cock Stick. All positions are closed. Mate, we've just made around four hundred and fifty mill. If that doesn't give you the fattest boner since prom night nothing will!' There was sheer joy in his voice.

'Christ alive! You've done it? It's your trades that have the moved the stock back up? You, my friend, are the man!' I tried to hide my excitement from those around me but fortunately they were too absorbed by their screens to notice.

'Tell me something I don't know! I might even be able to be hang out with you losers a bit more now that you're no longer paupers! Anyway, Skid Mark, party at my gaff in Sussex this weekend for the whole gang – come as soon as you finish work tonight. We have got some major fucking celebrating to do!'

Before I could say anything, Colum terminated the conversation. What he had done was nothing short of genius. He had crystallised our gains on all the bets we'd taken against Geldlust at what looked like exactly the right moment. I decided to follow suit in my own small way. I walked out of Geldlust and over to Liverpool Street station and used one of the public telephones there to call up my five pals who'd placed the spread bets on for me the week before. I told them all to close their Geldlust positions before midday and even mentioned a 'Christmas bonus' because we'd smashed it so dramatically; it seemed the least I could do. As I brought to a hasty end my conversation with Aunt Marge, which had been going on far too long due to her keenness to know whether I'd been wearing the scarf she'd knitted me, I calculated that these side bets alone would have netted me somewhere around £2 million. When I got back to the office and saw that the price of gold futures was still trading at around $1,650 I knew that I was a now a wealthy man, even excluding the vast gains Colum had accrued. If we got away with this I'd never have to even think about working for the man ever again. Christ, I'd be able to hire a couple of lingerie models just to spread the Marmite on my morning toast.

At midday we had a repeat performance of what had occurred five hours before. Groups gathered around the working computers and we waited. The announcement that flashed up at precisely 12.00 GMT was greeted by groans across the trading floor. Geldlust had agreed to be bought by the State of Saxony, which had already piled into the market and increased its stake to almost 36 per cent. Geldlust were being acquired at €25 a share but, more importantly, now had a very rich owner that would not be susceptible to spurious gossip about imminent bankruptcy. This had long been rumoured to be the State of Saxony's ambition and meant that Geldlust was effectively being nationalised. It had been previously suggested that the more conservative members of Geldlust's board had sought this outcome and that the federal government had been pushing for it too. They must have seen the recent troubles as the perfect opportunity to buy Geldlust on the cheap. Hell, they might have even purposely stood back and allowed the situation to worsen so as to get what they wanted. Of course, it was horrific news for everyone on the trading floor. We all knew that the square-heads in Saxony had no truck with the overpaid investment bankers in London who failed year in year out to make a decent return on equity. Now it was a question of when, not if, Geldlust's City operations would be dramatically cut down to size.

I looked around me at the nervous faces of my soon to be ex-colleagues and felt nothing but shame and guilt. These guys were all going to lose their jobs because of me and my gang. The joy at my imminent wealth was replaced by a sickening feeling of treachery. I couldn't look my colleagues in the eyes a moment longer. I had to leave this mausoleum. The stench of death was overpowering.

I stood up unsteadily, feeling hollow and nauseous, and barged my way through the throngs of people staring at the screens, my head bowed. As I approached the exit I sensed a familiar presence. I could feel a pair of eyes burning into the back of my head. I turned round and saw Richard staring at me. His face was bright red and he didn't blink. I turned my head away from my silent accuser and pushed my way through the glass doors towards the lifts. I knew that he was still glaring at me as the lift doors closed.

I'd never seen such hatred in a man's face.

Fifteen

Colum's manor house, West Sussex
Saturday, 11 December, 2.45 a.m.

BY 1 A.M. THE MUSHROOM tea was kicking in with a vengeance and the lunatics were well and truly in charge of the asylum. Colum was stomping around his huge atrium like some latter day Caligula, his crazed eyes looking as if they might pop out of his vast blotchy face at any minute. The entire bottom half of his pudgy nose was caked with high quality cocaine and he was drenched from head to toe in toxic sweat. Obnoxiously loud trance music was blaring out of his top-of-the-range Bang and Olufsen speakers and even though his feet seemed to be hitting the ground at fairly regular intervals it would hardly qualify as dancing – he looked more like someone directing traffic at Spaghetti Junction. If George Michael's claim that 'guilty feet have got no rhythm' was correct, then Christ only knows what sort of depraved nastiness that drug-crazed degenerate had been up to.

John's inability to dance was even more apparent. He was throwing shapes like a has-been newsreader on *Strictly Come Dancing*. Still, what he lacked in ability he made up for in boyish enthusiasm. His hands were whirling round his head like the rotor blades of a helicopter in a tailspin and he had such a gurn on that when he swung his head round we all had to duck his protruding chin. Rachel was somewhat more understated and little betrayed the fact that she was buzzing like a fridge other than the vacant grin plastered all over her sweet face. Meanwhile, Fergus stood with his back to the wall surveying the scene with a contented smile, tapping his foot in a mildly self-conscious manner. For the first time in weeks, he looked at peace with the world . . . which was surprising considering the arsenal of mind-wrenching narcotics he'd gamely consumed.

The evening couldn't have gone better. By about 8 o'clock we had all assembled at Colum's Tudor manor house, a few miles outside the West Sussex town of Petworth. Colum had pulled out all the stops for this particular shindig – a Michelin-starred chef had been hired to prepare our seven-course meal and the youngest wines we drank were still considerably older than the elegantly wasted guests who sat around Colum's immense oak table. We were served by two beautiful waitresses wearing preposterously short skirts and Colum insisted on slapping their pert buttocks whenever they came within reach. After our delectable dinner we smoked the finest Cohibas money could buy and drank a vintage port that had apparently been Winston Churchill's favourite tipple. Inevitably, a silver tray with dozens of fat lines of Colombia's finest export was passed around after the cigars. They were aggressively snorted by all the diners – most notably Colum who consumed two with each nostril and then started shouting insane gibberish at the ceiling whilst beating his chest like an enraged gorilla. For a moment I thought he'd genuinely lost it but a sly wink across the table put my mind at rest.

A couple of important announcements had been made after dinner. First, Colum gave us his final calculation of our 'winnings'. He said that each of us around the table had personally made £5 million from our scam. He neglected to mention how much he and his fund had made but it must have been a handsome multiple of our combined winnings. Still, I wasn't complaining – I now had enough money to leave banking and set about enjoying life free from the suited drudgery that I'd forced upon myself. After Colum's gleefully received news Fergus stood up. His eyes were once again moist and his voice was strained. The silence around the table added to the poignancy of his words.

'You know that I'm no good at this kind of thing. Never have been, never will be, but . . . I just can't express what this all means to me. I know we've all made a few quid but more than that we took revenge on the fuckers who killed my girl . . . and *we* got back at those fucking banksters! This is biblical, this is mythical . . . this is inspirational . . .'

The MDMA that had been passed around after the nozz-bag was clearly adding a poetic element to Fergus's diatribe. '. . . and before I stop my bullshit, I just want you all to know that I really do fucking love you guys . . . and that's got nothing to do with the drugs, honest!' Colum coughed theatrically after that last claim and we all shared a jaw-clenched titter.

'That's it – you're not getting any more. Just remember, act as normal as you possibly can over the next weeks. Don't give anyone any excuse to suspect us and we'll all be fine. And don't forget, if any of us do get questioned just plead the fifth. They'll probably try to turn us against each other . . . that's a trick they always pull to garner a confession. So, on the very off chance one of us gets done, please don't take the others with you. There, that's it – let's *fucking* party!' We all cheered. I hadn't seen such exuberance from Fergus in over a decade.

After Fergus's impassioned musings Rachel stood up unsteadily and added her tuppence worth. Her attempt to communicate was made marginally more complicated by the fact that she appeared to be frothing at the mouth and because she seemed to want to deliver her speech in a rare Latvian dialect. She was clearly making the most of her pink ticket.

'I just wanna say . . .' There was a worryingly long pause. Rachel momentarily appeared confused as to what exactly it was that she wanted to say. Her eyes were lolling around in her head like two pickled eggs on a chippy's counter and she was swaying precariously from side to side. 'I just wanna say . . .' This time there was a collective elongated 'yesss' from her impatient audience. I'm sure that just then one of her eyes rolled forward and the other back, temporarily leaving us with nothing but white. It looked momentarily as if she'd been possessed by the devil and was about to start projectile-vomiting green bile. Finally, she gathered herself and screamed: 'I just wanna say that . . . *we fucking did it!*' Her incisive declaration received a smattering of relieved applause. However, that was not all she had to say; we weren't going to get away with it so easily.

'And we showed those wankers . . . we showed Geldlust . . . they can't treat our Bridget like that . . . banks like that shouldn't be allowed to get away with it. Somebody had to show 'em and we fucking did . . . we showed 'em!'

It was at about that point that I felt like reminding her and Fergus that we'd all just made a shitload of cash from this 'altruistic' attempt to see justice done for Bridget and the 'little people'. But in a rare moment of restraint I decided to say nothing and instead pretended to listen to Rachel's garbled gibberish.

She continued talking nonsense for several minutes. At one point I could have sworn I heard her mention baba ganoush in the same sentence as John Maynard Keynes, so God only knows what was going through her addled mind at that juncture. She looked as though she might go on for ever so it was a relief when Colum finally sneaked up behind her and placed his hand over her mouth. After initially looking as if she was about to be raped by a troll, which probably wasn't so far from the truth, she pushed his arms away and said in a surprisingly lucid way: 'Oh yes, and we have to thank Colum for putting on this great party. What a fucking spread! I know sometimes he's a dick but we all love him really. So here's to you, Colum.'

She raised her glass and we all clinked each other. Whilst we all toasted Colum, Rachel turned round and gave him a theatrical sloppy kiss which she instantly regretted when he stuck his white crusty lizard tongue into her unsuspecting mouth. She spat out her wine, threw the rest over Colum's head and began chasing him around the table, and the rest of us fell about laughing. Madness then descended upon us all.

It was at about 6 a.m. that Colum revealed once again that he was a gentleman of true class and distinction. I was dancing very poorly next to him when suddenly a gangrenous odour hit my nostrils with such aggression that I momentarily felt that I'd descended into the ninth circle of hell. I looked around in almost comic disbelief to see if anyone else was experiencing this horror show when I caught Colum's gleeful eye and lunatic grin. The fat fuck had just unleashed a sulphurous floor clearer of biblical proportions. One by one my fellow revellers caught a whiff and each in turn looked around in horror, as if Dracula's coffin had been opened. Upon seeing our accusing looks Colum screamed out in his jarring Aussie drawl, 'Oh Christ! I've got the turtle head . . . oh fuck! I think I might have followed through,' and then fell to the ground in a fit of hysterics. I decided to make my excuses and leave ten minutes after that unpleasantness. Colum had just got out his high-powered air rifle and was talking animatedly about killing a few squirrels – 'They're just rats with good PR' he slurred after Rachel had objected on humanitarian grounds. He wanted us all to join him on his shooting spree, which was going to be livened up with a bottle of poppers and a wrap of ketamine. Whilst the thought of Colum's bizarre game was mildly tempting I took the easy and undoubtedly safer option and stumbled upstairs to my bedroom. I closed the door behind me and fell on to my bed feeling that all was well with the world.

Unfortunately, all was not well with the world.

'Mate, I slept like a baby . . . puked up twice, crapped my pants and woke up screaming for mummy!' roared Colum when I asked him how his night had been, and his glassy reptilian eyes and blotchy face betrayed the fact that his statement probably wasn't too far from the truth. In fact, I doubted if he'd had any kip at all. I'd heard him shooting away for hours just underneath my window as I chewed away on my pillow in a vast four-poster bed. I'd also bumped into him in the corridor on the way to an early morning piss. He'd claimed that he too was just heading to the bathroom 'to lay some cable' but there was something suspicious in his manner. He had definitely been up to something.

It must have been close to 10 a.m. when I'd finally succumbed to sleep and I only managed a couple of hours of jaw-grinding, restless slumber. I had another leprechaun dream and this time the little green fuckers had turned into skull-faced monstrosities who were chasing me around London leaping from building to building and cackling like witches. It was terrifying and I awoke with a start at around midday, covered in sour sweat. The sheets were soaking wet, I could barely open my gummy eyes and my throat felt like a crusty wank sock that had been used to clean a pub ashtray. I put my cupped hand to my mouth and exhaled. My breath would have made a camel with a fifty-a-day habit baulk.

After a few minutes of pitiful self-loathing I decided to venture downstairs for some breakfast. I stumbled into the kitchen and was immediately welcomed by the instantly recognisable stench of skunk. Colum was leaning back in his throne staring out of the window into the grey day that awaited us. He was nursing a Stella and smoking a Camberwell Carrot of alarming proportions.

He turned round slowly and stared at me for a few seconds with an insane glare in his eyes. It was almost as if he didn't recognise me. After cracking his oft-used baby gag he paused for an unnaturally long time. Finally, he held aloft the joint and, with a bizarre approximation of a Californian drawl, said: 'Wake and bake, baby. Wake and bake. A whole new way of looking at the day.'

I could see that getting any sense out of Colum that morning wasn't going to be easy.

Slowly but surely we were joined by our dissolute comrades-in-arms. John shuffled in first looking like a skinny Fred West after a dodgy day at the office. He was deathly pale and his eyes seemed to have more red than white in them. He was followed by a dribbling Rachel who looked like Ken Dodd on a bad hair day. She mumbled a few indecipherable words before sitting down and sipping her orange juice in complete silence. Finally, Fergus marched in. As ever, he looked annoyingly together and his booming 'good morning' to the war-ravaged refugees huddled around the table merely confirmed his status of apparent invincibility.

There were a couple of rounds of tea and toast peppered with some croaky post-party analysis and complaints about our debilitating hangovers. After I described my comedown as being 'eleven out of twelve on the Richter scale' John piped up, 'Well, I think we deserve to celebrate because what we did was a genuine achievement!' We all stared at him for a few seconds, mildly amused at his robotic pronouncement.

Fergus's soft lilting Scottish accent broke the silence that, as always, followed one of John's semi-autistic statements. His quiet, authoritative voice had a worrying edge to it. 'Well, let's not all give each other blow jobs just yet.'

A few seconds of stunned disbelief followed. The temperature in the room seemed to go up a degree or two. Why the hell was Fergus trying to piss on our strawberries? Even in our befuddled state it was clear that he had something on his mind. I felt my heart quicken. We all turned to stare at him.

'What are you talking about, Fergus? We've just shot the fucking lights out, mate,' said a bemused Colum.

'No, I've been thinking . . . I think we've just started something here and there's a lot more to go. Look, we've got these fuckers on the ropes. The market's going to be jittery for a few weeks after what's just happened to Geldlust. Everyone's looking around for the next bank that might be in trouble. We now know exactly how to take a bank down and we can easily do it again. We've got more money to play with and this team is unbeatable. We are going to shake up the fucking *world*!' As he spoke he was becoming increasingly agitated, directing his challenging glare from one member of the group to the next, jabbing his finger at each of us in turn.

Nervous glances were exchanged around the table. I couldn't believe what I was hearing and nor, it appeared, could anyone else. We had just pulled off the bank job of the century yet Fergus wasn't satisfied. If this wasn't an insane moment of hubris I didn't know what was. Finally, I broke the silence.

'Fergus, you've got to be fucking joking. We try this again and we *will* get nicked. Let's quit while we're ahead.' My voice had a pleading tone to it. I didn't want this tomfoolery to go any further.

'Bullshit! We can do this again and we're going to do it again.' Fergus definitely wasn't going to take no for an answer. He continued: 'Look, what we've done is just the dummy run for the main event . . . and this time we are going to go all the fucking way. Geldlust is just a pissant little German outfit but what worked with it will work with a bigger bank. I happen to have been talking to a couple of senior guys at Citigroup and with their help we're gonna bring it down. And Colum . . . guys . . . we're going to make so much money with this one that it will make our recent earnings look like small change.' Fergus stared at us defiantly, daring each of us to contradict him. We looked amongst ourselves for someone to challenge him but no one stepped up to the plate.

Again, I chose to break the silence. 'Listen, Fergus, are you on any special medication we should be aware of? This is fucking madness, mate.' I desperately wanted to make light of the situation. An optimistic part of me prayed that this was just an elaborate wind-up but I knew in my heart of hearts that it wasn't.

'Bullshit! We are going to do this. This is all-out war and we're going to take on the big boys of capitalism. You're either with me or against me and I want you to know that I'm not taking any *fucking* prisoners here.' There was something seriously threatening about those last words. What exactly did he mean? My paranoia was beginning to grow. My heart was pounding like a bass drum. I realised that Fergus had been planning this for days, probably weeks. Suddenly, John spoke.

'I'm with you, Fergus. If you've got another inside man, I don't see why we can't do this again.' John had always sucked up to Fergus. It had been Fergus who'd first taken him under his wing at Cambridge and John looked up to him like a younger brother. He was the weak link in the chain. Fergus must have known that he could rely on his support.

'Good on you, John . . . that's the spirit. Now, Rachel, you want to get your own back on firms that treat their employees like dirt and then throw them away, don't you? You want to wake the world up to what's really going on, don't you?' Rachel looked around for support but only found three sets of bleary eyes awaiting her response.

'Erm, I'm not sure, Fergus . . . I mean, haven't we avenged Bridget now?' she stuttered, clearly confused. She looked at me after she'd asked her question as if hoping for confirmation that she'd said the right thing. I tried to reassure her with a broken smile and a jerky nod of the head.

'Maybe, but what about all the other Bridgets out there? The millions who've suffered because of the banks? I'm going to show you all what I want us to do later this week and I think you'll all come round to my way of looking at things. In fact, I think you'll see that you have no real choice here.' Again, there was something extremely menacing about Fergus's tone. The knots in my stomach were multiplying by the second. Rachel nodded her head slowly and deliberately. Finally, Colum spoke.

'Well, if you can convince me we can make another huge score and that the risks are minimal then I'm in. We've got a winning formula, so I don't see why we can't use it again.'

Christ! It looked like everyone was up for it. Maybe they were just trying to placate an overbearing Fergus? I seriously hoped so. Surely Colum and Rachel realised this was madness? Perhaps they were just buying some time in the hope that Fergus would later see the error of his ways. Maybe they were scared by his not-so-subtle threats. At last I heard myself speak.

'Oh, for fuck's sake! Well, I suppose if you're all in I've got no choice, but this better be watertight because I ain't going to prison over this horseshit!' In reality, I was just responding to Fergus's thinly disguised threats and pretending to go along with his crazy scheme for the time being. I hoped with all my heart that he would eventually realise that it was the chemicals in his system that were doing the talking, and that he'd get off his power trip when the mid-week blues kicked in.

Fergus beamed from ear to ear. 'I knew I could count on you guys. Let's meet up next Friday to discuss Operation Grizzly . . . and believe me this is going to make Yogi look like a two-bit bank heist.' He slammed both meaty palms on the table to emphasise the point.

As we all nervously exchanged semi-smiling glances I couldn't help but feel a horrible sense of foreboding. There was a dark hole in the pit of my stomach.

I wondered whether we were all just about to sign our own death warrants.

Part Three

Part Three

'Recent popular demonstrations, from the Middle East to Israel to the UK, and rising popular anger in China – and soon enough in other advanced economies and emerging markets – are all driven by the same issues and tensions: growing inequality, poverty, unemployment, and hopelessness . . . So Karl Marx, it seems, was partly right in arguing that globalisation, financial intermediation run amok, and redistribution of income and wealth from labour to capital could lead capitalism to self-destruct' – Nouriel 'Dr Doom' Roubini (one of the only people who correctly predicted the financial crisis), 15 August 2011.

Sixteen

Financial Services Authority subsidiary office,
Moorgate
Tuesday, 14 December, 12.05 p.m.

RACHEL GATHERED HER THINGS AND walked towards the lifts, studiously avoiding eye contact with her diligent colleagues. She'd already informed her secretary that she was off to have a two-hour lunch with a potential witness vital to a serious fraud investigation and her secretary had, as always, believed her. Rachel was a little unsteady on her feet. She was still feeling the after-effects of the weekend's debauchery. She'd had another ugly argument with Darren on Sunday and she spent Monday pretending to work whilst she read all the weekend press reports about Geldlust's spectacular fall. She had been horrified to see that there was already some speculation about Geldlust's being the victim of a 'bear raid' and had been feeling steadily worse ever since. Her paranoia was beginning to whisper sweet nothings in her ear ever more frequently. Unfortunately for her, she knew all too well that there was only one thing more horrific than 'teary Tuesday' . . . and that was 'weepy Wednesday'.

She left the FSA City office in Moorgate and walked towards Liverpool Street station. It was bitterly cold and she regretted the short dress she was wearing. She pulled her midnight blue Yves Saint Laurent coat, a throwback to the days when she'd been a high-flying stockbroker working at Geldlust, tightly around her. She still felt chilled to the bone. She passed a Pret A Manger already filling with hungry bankers and quickened her step in case some former colleague recognised her and began a tiresome conversation about her humiliating career change . . . a step down she was still livid about. She still couldn't quite comprehend how or why she'd found herself working for a pittance with a bunch of dull automatons whose lack of ambition was only matched by their ineffectiveness. She blamed quite a few people for her fall from grace but, so far, only some of them had been punished.

Rachel smiled grimly to herself as she thought about the obnoxious ex-colleagues at Geldlust who were going to find themselves looking for a new job soon . . . a humiliation she herself had experienced two years before. It would be a genuine pleasure witnessing their demise. Sometimes the depth of her anger surprised her, as did the joy she took in hurting those who wronged her. Her smile grew broader as she contemplated her new wealth and how those riches had come from the same scam that had condemned the pricks at Geldlust. She'd made almost a million from her side bets, but the real pay day would come next year when she would be able to access the winnings that Colum's fund had generated. Then the fun would really begin. Her high heels clattered on the pavement and she once again cursed her impulsive decision not to take a taxi. Still, she was almost there now and she felt a wave of relief envelop her.

As she turned the corner into Finsbury Circus she thought she spied him again. Between the throngs of lunch-hour office workers, about fifty feet behind her, was a man in a woolly hat, a scarf and an overcoat. The thick grey scarf was piled up around the man's neck and together with the black beanie left only his eyes and nose exposed to the elements. It was cold but hardly cold enough to justify such extreme measures. This man clearly didn't want to be recognised. She had felt his presence before and not only today. She shivered, and this time it wasn't just the December chill.

After hurriedly circling the eastern arc of Finsbury Circus Rachel decided to take action. She'd heard Bridget talk about seeing a figure in hat and scarf following her a week or two before her death. Rachel had assumed then that it was merely coke paranoia but now she wasn't so sure. Her mind went into overdrive. Maybe Bridget hadn't killed herself? Maybe she'd been in trouble with someone? The questions were making her ever more nervous about the mysterious man and she had to know who he was. There were lots of people around so she figured she would be safe. She turned right towards Liverpool Street and after about forty feet darted up the six steps to someone's front door and backed into the doorway. She'd now be able to see her stalker as soon as he turned the corner.

Rachel waited. Then she waited some more. She hardly dared breathe. She felt her heart pound against her tight chest. Nothing. Her breathing was rapid and shallow. Suddenly there was a loud noise behind her, and her heart leapt into her mouth. She looked around, panic-stricken. There was an enraged old spinster at the front bay window glaring at her. She knocked violently on the window again and flapped her hand to shoo Rachel away. Rachel breathed a sigh of relief, gave the wizened old crow the finger and marched off. She continued to look over her shoulder every few seconds but the figure was nowhere to be seen. Either her stalker had realised she'd seen him and stopped following her or he'd come round the corner at exactly the moment she was being shooed away and withdrawn back into Finsbury Circus. Or had the whole thing just been the product of her fetid brain's post-party didginess?

After another few minutes of speed-walking and regular glances over her shoulder Rachel finally reached the Great Eastern Hotel – the Andaz, as it was now called. In seedy days gone by the rooms had been available to rent by the hour and it had been an infamous shagging parlour amongst a certain breed of stockbroker – the kind who didn't think twice about engaging in a lunchtime threesome with high class hookers and then chairing a board meeting back at the bank. Nowadays, after its 1999 revamp, it was a far classier joint and even the cheapest rooms didn't leave you much change from £300. As she walked up the stairs into the hotel she turned round to check one last time whether she was still being followed. She scanned the crowded street and saw no one. Had she imagined the whole thing?

After a while she turned round and pushed her way through the revolving doors. She gingerly approached the reception desk and asked the pretty woman behind it which room her husband, Mr Smith, was staying in. She was aware that it wasn't the most original false name in the world but it was the one they'd agreed upon.

'Oh, Mr Smith has just arrived. It's room 308. Third floor, on the left.' Rachel couldn't help but notice the faintest flicker of a smile on the receptionist's face. She felt a flush of anger but chose to ignore it. This was no time to draw attention to herself.

As Rachel approached the lifts, her heart began to quicken. What she was about to do was wrong on so many levels. She had to throw caution to the wind. This was not the moment to be weak.

Once in the lift, she pressed the button for the third floor. She noticed that her finger was trembling as she did so. The lift doors eventually opened and she walked out into a plush corridor. She approached room 308 with a stiff and unnatural gait, stopped outside the door and steadied herself with some long, deep breaths. She closed her eyes for a few seconds, and then opened them and knocked loudly. After a brief pause she heard footsteps approaching. She took another deep breath.

The door opened and she walked in.

Seventeen

Alpha Max Hedge Fund, Mayfair
Tuesday, 14 December, 2.45 p.m.

COLUM WAS FLIRTING WITH SHARON again as was his wont after he'd had a few lunchtime sharpeners. He asked her for the eighth time that month if she'd like a ride . . . on his motorbike . . . and for the eighth time, with a forced titter, she politely declined. It looked as though Colum would once again have to satisfy his seemingly insatiable sexual requirements with Simone but, he thought, that wouldn't be such a bad thing – she always gave every performance 100 per cent, especially if he paid up front. She was also remarkably tolerant of his more esoteric sexual demands. He had just made the usual ribald aside about Sharon's sitting on something 'huge, red and throbbing' when a group of five suited serious-looking men walked into the office. There were two uniformed policemen behind them.

Colum knew immediately that these guys weren't selling cookies door to door and his heart skipped a beat. As one of them took out his ID showing that he was from the Financial Services Authority, Colum felt his stomach lurch. He took a deep gulp of air and asked in as nonchalant a way as possible what the problem was. Considering that he knew exactly what 'the problem' was and that he was painfully aware that he faced many years in prison if the FSA worked it out too, he was remarkably calm. But this wasn't the first time that the incompetents at the FSA had come over to investigate his remarkable investment track record. After the initial shock, what angered him most was the horrifying realisation that he'd have to cancel his upcoming 4.30 with Simone. That someone dared stand in the way of his afternoon of carnal depravity transformed his initial fear into tetchy anger.

When he had confirmed that he was indeed Colum Boyd, the principal shareholder of Alpha Max, the head honcho of this group of pinheads – a certain James Montague – explained their presence.

'Mr Boyd, we have received a tip-off that your fund has engaged in some illegal activities with regard to the recent demise of Geldlust Bank. The LSE's records clearly show that your fund has profited handsomely from numerous different types of trades that were made just days before Geldlust went under and we are in possession of a warrant permitting us to search your premises – both your office and your various homes.' James Montague had clearly rehearsed his little speech and finished it with a smile as if pleased he hadn't tripped up over any of the words.

Sharon was staring at them with utter disbelief. Colum sensed her panic and put a comforting hand on her shoulder. He bent down and whispered, 'Don't worry, it's all fine,' and felt strong and authoritative as he did so. He then turned round to speak to the invading party knowing that Sharon would be looking up at him, admiring his coolness under pressure.

Little did Colum know that Sharon couldn't have cared less about the FSA raid's possible impact on Alpha Max's appalling boss – a man she had considered unbearable almost from the moment she'd first met him. However, she was smart enough to realise that this development was detrimental to her chances of getting another £50,000 Christmas bonus. She hadn't put up with Colum's tiresome bullshit over the last eleven months for fun. In her mind's eye, she could see hundreds of Jimmy Choo shoes and Gucci handbags slipping away from her.

'Well, Mr Montague, I guess if the boys in blue are here then you guys must mean business. You are, of course, welcome to all our records, and please feel free to interview any of the lads seated in there. If you don't mind I'll tell them first what's happening . . . you're welcome to listen in, if you'd like.' Colum felt some of his usual chutzpah flowing back into his system. You can't keep a good man down, he thought as he strode through the double glass doors into the open-plan office. These arse bandits were not going to present any significant challenge. James Montague rushed to keep up with his surprisingly ebullient quarry.

All five of Colum's junior partners were already staring in his direction as he waltzed into their section. Every one of them had long understood that something like this would happen at some point. A couple of the smarter guys had been aware of the recent Geldlust trades and knew what this was going to be about before Colum opened his mouth. Again, there was a general gnashing of teeth as Colum's loyal workers realised that their much-anticipated Christmas bonuses would undoubtedly be put on hold until the matter was cleared up.

'Guys, we've got a situation here. For some reason these guys think that we've been up to no good. Of course, they're mistaken. They've apparently had a tip-off, almost certainly from a jealous rival, and they just want to check that everything's kosher. Please don't panic and cooperate with them in every way possible. There, that's it.'

Feeling more confident with every passing second, Colum turned to James Montague. 'OK, that's them sorted. So, what can I personally do for you other than give you all my passwords?' His initial anxiety was dissipating rapidly as he took control of the situation. He was almost enjoying the whole experience.

'Well, I'm afraid, Mr Boyd, that you're going to have to accompany us to our offices to be formally interviewed. But before we do that I just wondered if I could ask you quickly what your reaction to these accusations is?' James Montague removed a brown Moleskine notebook from his breast pocket and flipped it open.

Colum took a deep breath and rattled off a spiel that he'd had to deliver several times before during his career.

'Look, we do not sail close to the wind at my firm. You will find no evidence of wrong-doing because there is none. We have a great track record here simply because we do our research and we work fucking hard. In this particular case, we analysed the publicly available information about Geldlust and became concerned about its ongoing exposure to the sub-prime issue. You will find some spreadsheets and graphs on my computer showing this analysis.' He had, of course, destroyed any evidence of the doctored letters and the false graphs that had been produced. He felt reasonably confident that he'd get away with this scam . . . as he always had. 'Once we'd discovered that there was no way in hell that Geldlust was going to be acquired by anyone other than the State of Saxony we knew that there was only one direction its shares were headed. We were, if anything, just too good.'

Colum smiled broadly as he uttered these final words. Such was his capacity for self-delusion that he'd almost convinced himself that the dizzyingly profitable Geldlust trades were the legitimate result of his planet-sized brain and God-like judgement. He'd once told a bored model he was trying to seduce at a Fashion Week party that he'd got a starred first at Cambridge and run a marathon in under three hours. By the time he was taking her home both claims had become so embedded in his twisted psyche that he found himself repeating them for years after-wards, only ceasing to do so after an unusually brave John had pointed out what utter crap he was talking. Colum had defended both claims for hours because he had genuinely believed they were true. Only after non-stop pestering from John did he finally concede that he 'might have exaggerated'. He had never forgotten John's unacceptable disloyalty and had promised himself that the little wanker would rue the day that he'd embarrassed Colum in front of his mates.

'Yes, your track record is very good . . . almost too good to be true. Well, if you're lying we *will* find out and if you're not then you'll be free to carry on as you are. Please come with us now.'

Colum gathered up his motorcycle jacket and walked towards the exit wondering which fucker had dobbed him in. As he left he promised himself three things: one, he'd get his lawyer involved ASAP; two, he'd tell the gang to call off Operation Grizzly tomorrow; and three, he'd tell Steve the secret he'd been guarding for over a month now.

Eighteen

John's flat, Camden
Tuesday, 14 December, 11.55 p.m.

JOHN'S MARKS & SPENCER'S READY meal lay half eaten on the coffee table in front of him. The watery fish pie hadn't agreed with him, but then little had since the weekend's hearty consumption of appetite-destroying pharmaceuticals. He lay on his moth-eaten couch watching mindless crap on the telly, only half taking it in. He felt anxious and full of self-loathing. He needed to do something to lift himself out of this funk, but what?

After a while the niggling got the better of him. As always, it was only a question of time. After a half-hearted internal debate he let his hand wander underneath the sofa and come up with the engraved Indian stash box. He sat up and opened it, his heart already beginning to beat faster in anticipation. Within it lay an impressive assortment of drugs. He selected the wrap of bright blue paper, opened it and poured some of the contents on to the mirror. He knew he'd regret this. He promised himself that he'd only have one line . . . at most two . . . three absolutely max. Expertly, he crushed the Charlie with a note and a credit card. He then made two perfect matchstick-sized lines and, after rolling up a twenty, aggressively snorted them both. He lay back in the sofa waiting for the familiar euphoria to envelop him. Within thirty seconds he could feel his heart pumping and a sly grin spread across his face. He was back.

John's mind began to race around at a thousand miles an hour. It was always flying but now it was going supersonic. John himself was impressed by the speed of the connections his flashing synapses were making. He analysed Operation Yogi and saw that it was beautiful. It had been so good to avenge Bridget – the only girl he'd ever loved. He then began to dissect the recent weekend and slowly but surely the rage powder began to live up to its name. He had logged every slight that Colum had delivered, every public put-down that had come his way. Colum had mentioned his 'schlort' on at least four occasions and once again alluded to his lack of success with women. He'd mentioned something about John's being 'unable to score in a three-shilling Kenyan brothel' and kept pointing out his ever-receding hairline. The more John thought about the fat, ugly fuck the more he clenched and unclenched his fists. After a while he stood up and walked jerkily to the long mirror in the corner of the room. He placed his feet shoulder-width apart and assumed the basic Kung Fu fighting pose – knees slightly bent and upturned fists by the side of his body. He closed his eyes and took some long, deep breaths through his nose. He tried to clear his mind of all the detritus that had built up over the week, to reach a Zen-like feeling of weightlessness. But one hideous image kept rearing its ugly head – the red, blotchy countenance of his age-old nemesis. Despite his best efforts Colum's gurning, grinning face kept on barging its way into his consciousness.

John's troubled mind wandered back to an especially humiliating fancy dress party in the second year at Cambridge. The theme had been superheroes and he had foolishly chosen to go as Wonder Woman. The decision to drop acid early on in the proceedings was, with hindsight, another grave misjudgement; an error that had been compounded by Batman/Colum's drunken decision to rip John's star-spangled pants off and shout to the assembled crowd of Spidermen and Catwomen, 'See, he really is a woman underneath the costume!' John remembered the hoots of laughter from the men and the looks of awkwardness from the women, who covered their mouths in embarrassment. He had run out on to the road, holding his exposed tackle with one hand and wiping away the tears with the other.

John began punching and kicking the air with the precision and expertise that eight years of hard study had taught him. He imagined smashing Colum's face in with every hit. After about ten minutes of furious shadow-boxing he found himself sweaty and breathless. He went back to his lonely sofa and pulled out his laptop, then grabbed two tissues from the box sitting on the table and reached under the sofa for the family-sized Nivea moisturizer that he kept there. He'd only bought it two weeks ago and it was almost empty. John felt another wave of self-loathing but quickly dismissed it. There was work to be done – serious work. He had just clicked on to YouPorn when he heard a knock on the door. His eyes widened with horror and his semi-boner immediately wilted away. There was another knock, and John thought he could hear muffled voices. He quickly stepped into his trousers and pulled a sweatshirt over his head before gingerly approaching the door. With as much false confidence as he could muster, he said: 'Hello, erm, can I help you, please?'

Then he heard the words that he'd been dreading for years.

'It's the police, Mr Roberts. Please open up right now or we will knock this door down. Best not to disturb the neighbours, eh?'

John's mind went into overdrive. His heart was racing and his breaths were short; he had to think damn fast but it was proving impossible. He was like a rabbit in the headlights. After a frantic hesitation that seemed like an eternity he said: 'OK, I'll just get some clothes on and be with you in ten seconds.' With that, he raced back to the sofa and scrabbled underneath for his drug box. This was just his personal stuff; he knew that there was no way the coppers would find his main hoard. He leapt to the window and poured the contents out on to the street four storeys below, then replaced the stash box and walked as calmly as he could back to the door.

When he opened it, four burly uniformed officers marched in, looking bemused at the state of John's messy student-style living room. They began, pulling up cushions and removing books from the shelves. John immediately regretted not having closed his laptop, which was showing a particularly gruesome scene involving a forty-something 'German MILF' having fun with some extremely large root vegetables. John heard some stifled giggles as one copper said to the others, 'Channel Five, I reckon.' The plain clothes guy, who introduced himself as Sergeant Gordon Baker, stayed by the front door to talk to him. He showed John the search warrant granting the police permission to enter his premises and then asked if he had anything in the house that he shouldn't have . . . 'apart from what's showing on that laptop, that is?' John blushed some more but replied that he didn't.

Sergeant Baker kept John in the corridor and chatted amiably with him about the police's suspicion that he had illegal narcotics in his flat. John's request to know why they harboured such a suspicion was quickly batted away. Still, he felt confident that they would not find the fourteen grams of cocaine, the forty or so Ecstasy tablets and the nine grams of ketamine that were carefully hidden inside a false can of baked beans at the back of one of the cupboards in the kitchen. He had bought the screw-up tin in Bangkok and it was so realistic that there was no way they'd find it. It weighed almost as much as a normal tin, had a seal that was undetectable and, if you opened it in the normal way, the top two thirds was actually filled with baked beans. Despite the paranoia-inducing cocaine he'd snorted John felt sure he was safe. Hell, it was clearly amateur night because these clowns hadn't even brought a sniffer dog.

After only three minutes John heard a shout from the kitchen that instantly turned his stomach to water – 'Sarge, I think we found it.' One of the policemen walked out holding the baked bean can in his latex-gloved hands. John's eyes widened with horror as, in front of him, the can was unscrewed and its illegal contents dropped into Sergeant Baker's hands. Sergeant Baker looked up at John and saw the debilitating fear written all over the poor lad's face. He almost pitied the balding weirdo. After a few seconds he trotted out a line that he had said countless times before.

'John Roberts, I am arresting you for breach of the Misuse of Drugs Act, 1970. You do not have to say anything, but it may harm your defence if you do not mention, when questioned, something which you later rely on in court. Anything you do say may be given in evidence.'

The words became meaningless background noise as John saw his secure future crashing into nothingness. Unlike the others, John hadn't accrued the capital to make lots of lucrative side bets. As things stood, Yogi had only earned him £120,000. Sure, he was due to get £5 million from Colum at some point but that wasn't going to materialise for at least six months and he was sufficiently cautious not to count his chickens – especially when that fat prick was involved. What was more, John still valued his job and the vague stability it represented in his chaotic life. Without it he would be just another small-time druggie loser whom no one would ever take seriously.

As he stood shivering in the corridor contemplating his bleak future, the one thing John knew with absolute certainty was that one of his friends had grassed him up.

I was startled awake by the horrible piercing ring of my home phone, and looked at the clock. It was 7.10 a.m. I'd taken the week off as holiday so there was no reason for me to be called on the landline at this ungodly hour. I scrambled around bleary-eyed trying to locate the offending item, regretting the two bottles of wine I had once again drunk on my own whilst watching TV into the small hours. It had become my mournful nightly ritual since Bridget's death. Eventually I located the source of the ear-splitting noise under a crumpled pile of clothes – one of many scattered around my bedroom. I sensed something was wrong even before I'd picked up the receiver.

'Steve, Steve . . . it's John. Look, I've just got out of the police station. I've been arrested. I'm going down, man . . . I'm fucking going down!' His voice was trembling with fear. I felt my heart quicken and the dull pounding in my head deepen. I had to think quickly, but my shrivelled brain needed at least two coffees before it would start functioning.

'What? What the fuck? Just a minute . . . call me back on

the Yogi mobile. Don't a say a fucking word on this phone, OK?' The sudden realisation that my own well-being was under threat cut through the fog of my hangover.

'No, it's fine. This is nothing to do with Yogi and I haven't said a word about that to the cops. This is to do with the police finding my fucking stash six hours ago.'

I breathed a huge sigh of relief. 'Shit! That's terrible!' I said, trying desperately not to let him hear how pleased I was that it was just his problem.

'I'm telling you, Steve, some wanker has grassed me up. No one, apart from the gang and maybe two or three others, knew where my secret stash was kept.' There was a long pause. I thought he might be crying. Then he said it: 'Mate, I think there's a rat in our group.'

I listened to myself breathe for a few seconds – the nervous, shallow breaths of a condemned man – before I answered with as much assurance as I could muster: 'Bullshit! Why the fuck would one of us want you nicked? You said there were people outside the group who knew about your famous baked bean tin.'

'Yeah, but I can't see why the hell they'd want to get me done – I haven't seen a couple of them for years. I think . . . I think someone in our gang wants all the cash for himself. They want me out of the way and you know exactly who I think it is . . . fucking Colum. That greedy prick has always had it in for me.' John spat out our supposed friend's name with genuine hatred. I had clearly underestimated the depth of the animosity between the two of them.

'Look, John, this is horseshit. You're putting two and two together and coming up with five. Quit hammering the bugle and stop getting paro, OK? Let's chat about this later . . . and please, please do not do anything stupid.'

'All right, but you're not going to convince me that it's not that fat bastard. Rachel's too nice, you're solid, and not only does Fergus like me, he needs me for Operation Grizzly. I'm going home now to think about this, but I know something's up.' I was left listening to the dialling tone.

I clicked the phone off, stared at the wall in front of me and tried to process the information. Who from the group would have done this? No one. There were a hundred and one reasons why the police could have found John's drugs. There was no possible reason why any of the gang would want John nicked. Our fates were all connected. If one of us got arrested it merely increased the chances of them squealing and bringing the whole gang down. No, John was undoubtedly spouting codshit. I decided to call Fergus to warn him about what was happening. Just in case, I rang his pay-as-you-go on my brick.

Before I'd even uttered a word, Fergus started talking. 'Skid Mark? So you've heard, yeah?' There was a tone of concern in Fergus's usually reassuring Scottish brogue.

'You mean about Jizz Stain?'

'No, about Cock Stick. He got done yesterday by the Fucking Shite Arseholes' – our subtle code for the FSA. 'They questioned him for almost six hours. He rang me at half past eleven last night and we chatted for over an hour. I thought I'd let you sleep and talk to you in the morning. In fact, I was just about to ring you.'

I couldn't believe what I was hearing. My frazzled brain was desperately trying to work out how much danger we were in. 'He hasn't said anything, has he?' My heart was racing even before he answered. My hands were trembling. Things were going horribly wrong.

'No, he's solid . . . I think. The thing is that the Shite Arseholes were apparently tipped off . . . and he's got it into his fat head that it's someone in the gang – which just has to be gash. Why would any of us shoot ourselves in the foot? I'm afraid he's insisting that this means Grizzly's on hold and he's probably got a point. I can't fucking believe it . . . I am gutted. I've been working on it non-stop since the party. I can't tell you how fucking gutted I am.' Fergus sounded genuinely livid. It was the second time in ten minutes that I had to feign concern.

'Operation Grizzly's off? Oh, that is genuinely upsetting, mate.' In fact, it was the best news I'd heard all year. If Fergus saw through my poor acting he wasn't letting on. I suspect that he was so wrapped up in his own anger that he was hardly listening to me anyway.

'Fucking tell me about it. We're still gonna do it though, mate, I tell you. We're gonna show the fucking world that people do get punished when they do wrong.' There was something seriously unhinged about his tone. Either the after-affect of Bridget's death or last weekend's debauchery was clearly playing havoc with his mind. 'Anyway, why did you mention Jizz Stain?'

I explained what had happened to poor John and, after a pause, mentioned John's suspicions that there was a rat in the group.

'That has to be baloney. I know it's not me and I'm sure it's not you . . . Cock Stick's been done and so has Jizz Stain. That only leaves Ring Piece, who isn't the type. What do you think?'

I took a deep breath and began explaining something that I'd been thinking about just before I'd called Fergus.

'Look, we have to consider all the possibilities . . . maybe Cock Stick did get done because of a random tip-off. I mean – he's made enough enemies in his time, and there are a hell of a lot of jealous competitors who have probably heard about the killing he made with Dog Shit plc. If someone's got to him then maybe he's squealing away . . . giving the bizzies anything he can think of . . . like Jizz Stain's dealing sideline. Anything to throw them off the scent. Anything other than Yogi, because he's the one who stands to lose most if that's discovered. You know he and Jizz Stain have always had a tricky relationship . . .' My voice tailed off. I could hardly believe what I was saying, but the more I thought about it the more sense it made. Colum and John really did hate each other.

'Mate, if you go down that route you might as well question what Jizz Stain's up to. He's the cleverest guy I know but by all accounts his drug habit's getting out of control. Apparently he's also short of cash. Who knows what the wee feller would do to make sure he gets the lion's share of the money? He also hates Cock Stick. Maybe he dobbed him in and Cock Stick's paid him back in kind?'

'Christ alive! You'll be telling me Ring Piece shot JFK next! Come on, mate, let's not get ahead of ourselves.'

'OK, but I'm telling you one thing: keep your wits about you because someone's up to something.' And with that he ended the call.

I stared into the middle distance. Some part of me knew that things were about to get a whole lot worse.

Nineteen

Camden
Wednesday, 15 December, 7.35 a.m.

JOHN FELT THE HAIRS ON the back of his neck prickle
again. He assumed it was the cold and let out a shiver.
A light drizzle fell on his head. He remembered the
good old days when he'd had sufficient hair to act as a
barrier against the elements, but those days were gone now,
and as a result of his own nervous tics, rather than the
relentless onslaught of middle age. God hadn't exactly dealt
John a wonderful hand yet he still managed to make things
worse for himself whenever possible. He wondered why
he needed to constantly score own goals when the other
teams were so much stronger than him. 'A rod for your own
back' Fergus had once called him, and events kept proving
him right.

He'd endured a terrible night and it still wasn't light yet.
The cops had got his number after approximately twelve

seconds – a nerdy middle-class professional with a sizeable drug habit. That was all. Not a dealer in any serious sense of the word and most certainly not a gangster. Apart from the embarrassment of being caught stroking one out to a wrinkly Fräulein with a penchant for genetically modified carrots he'd only been able to think about two things whilst being interviewed: was he going to lose his job and who was the wanker who'd grassed him up? If the answer to the first question was yes and he discovered the answer to the second, then the treacherous pig fucker would find out what a black belt karate expert can do with a single punch. Shit, that slimy cocksucker was going to look pretty damn stupid with no fucking teeth.

He'd been walking for almost forty minutes and he was almost home now. Not taking a taxi had been a good choice, he thought. He needed to clear his head. He needed to calm down. It was the first time he'd been in trouble with the law and it hadn't been an experience he'd like to repeat. Still, the interview had been fairly relaxed, all things considered. The cops hadn't tried anything too heavy and it was only when he'd had his fingerprints taken and his mouth swabbed for DNA for the second time that he remembered that he really was in big trouble. It took him thirty minutes just to fill in the numerous forms that the police required, and the subsequent hours he'd spent in the cells whilst they checked out his story and continued searching his flat had been mind-numbingly tedious – a short-lived taste of what might lay ahead.

Suddenly, he felt it again – the hairs on the back of his neck standing up. He was being followed. He responded to the realisation relatively calmly, his recent trials having sapped his reserves of shock and fear. He did nothing until he reached a crossroads. Then, as he turned the corner, he glanced around, and spied someone about seventy feet behind him. The figure was wearing a woolly hat, a thick overcoat and a scarf. The man had been staring at him but quickly averted his eyes on meeting John's. John walked on, his heart beating faster with each step. This bloke didn't look like a mugger. Either he was a copper or it was something more worrying. Despite the cold, John felt his back dampen with perspiration. What was happening to him? Why couldn't they just leave him alone? Why was life so difficult? Anger began to replace fear. Whoever this arsehole was, they'd chosen the wrong day to mess with him. John clenched his fists. He knew just how to handle this situation.

John turned right down a small lane that he'd been down a hundred times and pressed himself against the wall. There was no one else around. He waited and listened out for his stalker. He tried to steady his hasty breaths. After about ten seconds he heard the man's footsteps approaching. He readied himself. He clenched his fist tight and pulled his shoulder back. The stalker was just seconds away now. John took a deep breath and felt a strange calm envelop him. This arsehole was about to find out the true meaning of the word pain.

Suddenly the figure rounded the corner. John struck without a second's hesitation. His fist twisted in the air and landed perfectly on the man's nose. The man's eyes had widened in horror even before the punch had landed. John felt warm blood as soon as his hardened knuckles connected with the man's soft nasal cartilage. The man fell to the pavement, holding his face, and lay there for a few seconds, groaning. He then looked up and slowly removed his hands. Despite the blood streaming out of his nose and the woolly hat covering the top of his head there was something familiar about him. John had seen those eyes before. He blinked in disbelief. Suddenly it came to him. He couldn't believe it. He hadn't seen this loser for over a decade.

It was 'the gimp' . . . Richard fucking Stimp.

'So, you see – I think it's in your best interests if you tell me everything that's going on. I think you'll find that *I* hold all the cards.' Richard's slimy sneer was angering John more and more. He'd always hated the malicious little shit at Cambridge and Stimp had, if anything, become even more irritating with age – quite an achievement considering how high he'd set the bar whilst a student. His piggy little eyes, smug demeanour and the Matterhorn-sized chip on his shoulder made John want to hit him again, though he knew that wouldn't be the smartest move. The first punch might have been legally explicable even for a man who'd been barely an hour out of the cop shop, but to get away with a second smack would require a lawyer who made Johnnie Cochran look like Mr Bean.

'Maybe you're right, but I still would like to know who told you about my bust. Have you got friends in the police force or something?' John could barely control the rage that was bubbling up beneath the surface.

'How I came to know about your predicament is neither here nor there. What is both here and there is the fact that your firm won't take too kindly to finding out that their star employee is in fact a drug dealer . . . and, unfortunately, I will be forced to tell them unless you tell me everything that your pathetic little gang's been up to. I knew you twats were somehow involved in Geldlust's demise.'

There was a pleasing amount of blood still dripping from Richard's nose and his eyes were still glassy from the tears that a solid punch to the nose always produces. Yet after falling to the ground he had turned the tables remarkably quickly. He was hurt but he had been desperate not to show it. He knew John wasn't as bad as some of the other members of his gang, like Colum and Steve, but he'd still always hated him at Cambridge. He'd seen John and his so-called 'cool' pals laugh at him numerous times as he once again failed to pull some chick at yet another dreadful May Ball. It was galling that a fellow spod like John felt able to mock his amateur efforts to get into some pissed-up Sloane's knickers. He'd never forgotten the time John had passed him just as yet another girl had rejected his clumsy advances and muttered under his breath 'crashed and burned again' with a sly smile on his face. That passing comment still gnawed away at him years later.

There was a long pause after Richard's threat. The two men stood there staring at each other. Eventually John spoke up.

'So tell me, what can you offer me if I help you out?'

Twenty

Steve's flat, Old Street
Wednesday, 15 December, 11.15 a.m.

I SENSED THE LITTLE FUCKER long before he'd rung the
bell. His poisonous aura entered my house well before
he did. Initially, I thought that Mr Tibbs's puckered
arse was to blame but nothing on this sweet earth, not even
half a pound of mouldy Whiskas, could produce the aroma
that man's grotesque personality seemed to emanate. As I
shuffled towards the door, my every sinew begging me to
hightail it back to the living room, I readied myself for a truly
horrifying experience. If this wasn't Richard Stimp then it
was surely the skeletal scythe-wielding feller come to take
my corrupt soul to his fiery pit.

It was the gimp and he had a red, swollen nose. I gritted
my teeth and prepared for verbal combat.

'Christ alive. Just when you thought it was safe to open
your door . . .' I said in weary resignation, rubbing my

stubbly chin. Shaving, like showering, had taken a back seat since this whole shit storm had started.

'Hello, Steve.' Richard spat out the words with as much forced contempt as he could manufacture. 'I think it's time you and I had a chat.'

'And why on earth would I do that when I could be rubbing broken glass into my bell-end? You . . . despicable little wank stain.' It was an interesting choice of insult but I was running out of terms of abuse where this arsehole was concerned. It was getting to the stage where I would have to start reusing old ones.

'Look, you twat, Colum and John have been squealing like stuck pigs. I know everything about the number you pulled on Geldlust. You are going down . . . down to China Town.'

I don't know where the slimy little nonce had picked up that preposterous phrase but it was completely inappropriate this side of the Atlantic. Still, he could have divulged that particular piece of information whilst dancing an Irish jig and it still would have had the desired effect. My heart skipped several beats and it took all my self-control to avoid defecating in my silk boxers right there and then. But I couldn't let this little tosspot know that he'd got to me. I took my brave pills and tried to act as if he'd just made a passing comment about the weather.

'Child, I've seen some piss-poor bluffs in my time but this one takes the biscuit. Fuck me, I'd love a game of poker with you . . . I would make a fucking fortune! No wonder you never made it as a broker.' I was trying to take the battle to him, attack being the best form of defence and all that. Unfortunately, Richard was about to follow his right hook with a couple of nasty body blows.

'Well, if I'm bluffing how come I know all about the FSA investigation into Colum? Oh yeah, and how come I've been down at Kentish Town police station having a nice chat with John? That wiped the smile off your face, didn't it?'

I could feel all the blood drain from my face. My colon was rapidly filling up with a couple of litres of rusty water. It took all the strength I could muster not to squat down and show Richard why you should never have a chicken dhansak the night before being told you might be doing ten to fifteen. He knew about both screw-ups and they'd only happened yesterday. Things were going from bad to worse at warp speed twelve, but I had to keep playing the game.

'Mate, you've gone properly delusional now. I've got half a mind to section you. Still, I suppose it's understandable – you're an angry little man and I would be too if my jockstrap was a peanut shell and a rubber band. But please don't start bandying accusations around unless you wanna be picking up your teeth with broken fingers, OK?' I knew immediately that I had overplayed my hand but I couldn't back down now. I'd also come out with a threat that hadn't been heard since the early days of *Grange Hill*.

'Threats now, is it? Oh, I've definitely got you riled, haven't I? Your so-called mates are spilling the beans about you right now so they can reduce their own sentences. Pal, you'd better fight fire with fire or there's only going to be one serious loser in this game.' There was an increasingly smug assurance in Richard's manner that was causing me major concern. We'd had quite a few slagging matches over the years and I'd always outpunched him with ease . . . but not this time. Still, I couldn't let on that he had me on the ropes.

'God's teeth – who've you been taking your acting lessons off? Liz Hurley? Try again next year, son. Christ, to think that of the two hundred million sperm your retarded father sprayed into your poor mother the one that produced you beat the rest . . . God help us! Anyway, what is it you *think* I've done?' I was desperate to find out how much Richard knew. I was trying to talk in as calm a manner as possible but all the time I was wondering when the next flight to Rio was.

'It's not just the Geldlust job I know about. I know about what you get up to at the Black Cat in Frankfurt too. The coke, the prozzers and taking clients there. All unethical, illegal stuff. So, tell me – how would I know about these things if your so-called mates weren't squealing?'

Again, I felt like covering my front step with arse water. The Black Cat was Frankfurt's finest brothel. I'd first gone there in 2005 and it had blown my mind. A senior salesman, who was escorting me round the German client base, had told me that we should 'unwind' after a hard day's marketing. I thought he'd meant have a few beers and shoot a couple of games of pool . . . but I was about to be proved very wrong.

He meant *seriously* unwind. He got a taxi to drop us off at the edge of town in what appeared to be a normal residential street. My suspicions had been raised during the journey because Frank had had this weird smile plastered on his face the whole time. My imagination had been going into overdrive. We approached the largest house on the corner and Frank rang the bell. He had a muffled conversation in German with whoever it was behind the door and beckoned me over. As soon as we'd entered the house, everything became clear. Crystal fucking clear.

We were led into a plush hall by a statuesque Claudia Schiffer lookalike wearing some kind of hardcore S&M outfit – preposterously high heels, red leather basque, elbow-length red silk gloves; this girl wasn't mucking about . . . and nor were her friends lying around on the purple and pink satin cushions that were piled up against all four walls. I've seen some stunners in my time – perfectly proportioned teenage Eurotrash at Ibizan pool parties, cosmetically enhanced 'exotic dancers' in Miami and athletic goddesses at a Mayfair models shindig I'd once blagged my way into – but these women took things to a new level. I thought I was about to jet in my pants there and then and cursed the fact that I'd left the hotel with a loaded gun in my pocket. Having 'one in the chamber' meant that this was going to be a two-stroke manoeuvre if ever there was one . . . and one of those was taking it out of my pants.

Anyway, the experience ended predictably enough – a few bottles of shampoo, a couple of grams of ream sparkle and a torrid threesome with two chicks who looked like Helena Christensen and Naomi Campbell . . . and, of course, a wallet that was lighter to the tune of €4,000. I desperately hoped it would be a one-off. The thing is, though, that those kinds of experiences have a nasty habit of staying with you. The prospect of repeating such a pleasurable few hours claws away at your consciousness when you least expect it – over a Sunday roast with your parents or whilst listening to a presentation about carbon emissions. It was as if from then on it was for ever imprinted on my psyche and each subsequent visit left the image more permanently engraved. Back then I used to fly out to Frankfurt at least once a month on business and, despite my moral side's half-hearted protestations, I found myself heading over to the Cat every time I was in town. I started making up business trips just so that I could go there again. I became a pretty well-known client and because I sprayed the wonga around like some cracked-up lottery winner the girls loved me. Then I began taking clients there and the commission started rolling in. Turns out those buttoned-up Krauts can't get enough of a bit of hard-core. I justified the trips to myself by claiming that they were a good way of bonding with my customers. Of course, it was a load of contemptible horseshit – I just relished getting my rocks off with a bunch of brasses that made my average girlfriend look like Nora Batty.

The problem was that very few people knew about my dubious pastime. Admittedly, all the clients I took there did but they had no reason to dob me in because they'd be jeopardising their own careers if any of this came out. And everyone in the gang knew about it because I'd once foolishly told Colum about my 'hobby' after having hoofed enough nose candy to give Pablo Escobar the willies. Of course, he had immediately informed everyone else in the group without telling me and they had then proceeded to make piss-poor gags at my expense. Every time we passed a black cat on the street Rachel or Bridget would say something like 'I really love that black cat . . . you like the black cat, don't you, Steve?' It took me about three weeks to realise that something was up.

Since so few people knew about my esoteric predilection it looked as though Richard was telling the truth – maybe Colum or John or both of them were revealing everything bad that I'd got up to, trying to make out I was the wrong 'un and not them. It was now obvious that there was a rat in the pack – probably the same fucker who'd been outside my flat trying to freak me out, unless, of course, that was this twat. I pushed those thoughts aside and considered my poor parents – my loving mother and my seriously Christian father who had just suffered a heart attack. Whilst I didn't give two shits about the detrimental effect these revelations would have on my soon-to-be-over career I couldn't bear the thought of my dad's hearing about his whoremongering junkie son. The shock would kill him. And poor Aunt Marge would probably have a bleeding embolism. I didn't know what to say. Richard broke the silence.

'That shut you up, didn't it? I can't wait to see your face when I tell everyone about what you get up to in your spare time.' After a suitably long pause he spoke again. His voice was softer this time. It was as if he were suddenly keen to project an image of agreeableness . . . that really he had my best interests at heart. 'Look, your mates are grassing you up and you're going down one way or the other . . . so why don't you cooperate with us and we'll make sure that things are made easy for you?'

This was no time for subtlety, no time for witty quips and playful epigrams. After glaring at Richard for a few seconds I screamed 'FUCK OFF' and slammed the door in his face.

I stumbled back down the corridor.

It felt as though I was walking towards a firing squad.

Twenty-One

Fergus's flat, Brick Lane
Thursday, 16 December, 10.15 a.m.

FERGUS STARED AT THE WALL, his eyes sodden with tears. He sat on the edge of his bed, his elbows on his knees, holding his head in his hands. His toes were tapping nervously on the ground – they had been for two hours. Once again he hadn't slept a wink. He'd spent most of the night staring at the ceiling, feeling an unremitting sense of despair – wishing Bridget was by his side. For the fifth time that hour he picked up the T-shirt that she used to wear in bed and smothered his face in it. He closed his eyes and breathed in its sweet scent – the unmistakable smell of Bridget. He held the T-shirt to his face for several minutes and tried to control his frantic breathing. His mind kept going round in circles and nothing seemed to bring him any peace. Why had she left his life? Why was he alone now? There were no answers to the questions that plagued him.

He had thick black bags under his eyes, his cheeks were hollow and his formerly muscular chest was sunken. He had lost two stone since she'd died.

Suddenly, his home phone trilled and awoke him from his daze. After about five seconds he creakily raised himself up and stumbled the few paces to his bedside table. The phone kept ringing. He stared at it some more and then reached down and picked up the receiver. He held it to his ear and after a few more seconds said in as confident a fashion as he could, 'Yeah?' Despite his best efforts he still sounded like a broken man.

'Hi, Fergus. It's Rachel. Something . . . something terrible has happened. Can I come round? I . . . I really need to talk to someone. Could I come? Please?' Rachel's voice was strained and croaky. She kept sniffing. She'd obviously been crying. There was real desperation in her tone, and Fergus snapped out of the torpor he'd been wallowing in. He had to be sharp.

'Sure, come round straight away. It would be good to see you. Whatever it is, I'm sure we can sort it out together. Jump in a cab right now. There'll be a hot cup of tea waiting for you.' Fergus felt happy that he'd have some company and knew that Rachel's presence would be of real help to him too.

Rachel thanked him and Fergus replaced the receiver. He looked around and saw what a mess his flat had become: bins overflowing, dirty plates and mouldy mugs everywhere. He was usually so clean and tidy . . . one of the few repercussions of his brief army career. He'd spend the thirty minutes it took Rachel to reach him clearing the place up. He didn't want anyone to see how depressed he was. He wanted everyone to think he was on top of things. He needed them to believe he was the same old reliable Fergus that he'd always been.

Rachel arrived, as expected, half an hour later. Her face had the red, puffy look of someone who'd been crying all night. Fergus hugged her at the doorway and motioned her in. She walked past him, sniffling, and he poked his head out and scanned the street in both directions. There was no one around.

Once settled at his kitchen table with a steaming cup of tea Rachel began to talk. Tears occasionally welled up in her eyes and she had to take a gulp of air every few seconds. Her head was bowed and she looked intently at the top of the table as she spoke. 'So . . . Darren's gone and left me. He's taken the kids and he's gone to stay with his parents in Cheshire. He found out . . . he found out I was having an affair.' Rachel raised her head and stared defiantly at Fergus. His shock was obvious.

'You . . . you're having an affair?' Fergus's mouth fell open. He almost looked as if he was about to laugh, such was his utter disbelief.

'Yes. Why are you so surprised? These things happen. You knew Darren and I haven't been getting on. What are you saying . . . that I'm just some frumpy mum?' She was genuinely annoyed at the obvious incredulity etched on Fergus's face, but she had expected this reaction. She'd always hated being the unsexy girl in the group. She'd always hated how Bridget had stolen the limelight. From Cambridge onwards, whenever men approached Bridget and Rachel she'd always known which of them they'd come to talk to. Sometimes, when a man gathered up the nerve to offer them a drink at some City bar, Rachel would explain to the unfortunate chap that her friend's name was Bridget and that no, she wasn't interested. Darren had been the only one who had said quick as a flash, as if he really meant it, that he had actually come up to talk to Rachel. The joy she'd felt following that oh-so-rare occurrence went some way towards explaining why she'd married him. Later on, during one of her many arguments with Darren, he had informed her that he had, in fact, wanted to chat up Bridget but had been put on the back foot by Rachel's prickly attitude. Their entire relationship, it seemed, was based on a lie.

'No, I'm not saying that. I'm just surprised, that's all. I don't suppose it's with anyone I know, is it?' Fergus was keen to return to conciliatory mode. A part of him felt flattered that she'd chosen him in her hour of need and he wanted to uphold his part of the bargain. Looking shell-shocked by the revelation that Rachel was a sexual being who'd somehow managed to attract a lover was neither kind nor helpful.

'Yes, you know him. You know him quite well.'

Fergus's eyes widened. He looked up at the ceiling, obviously trying to work out who it was. After about five seconds a big smile broke out on his face and he said: 'It's fucking Steve, isn't it? The dirty dog! I can't believe it!' He was smirking now, slapping the top of the table with his hand.

'No, not Steve. It's . . . it's Colum.' Rachel was clearly embarrassed by this admission. She knew that Fergus would have assumed that their old friend's well-known predilection for debauched sex with ladies of the night would put off most sensible women. Indeed, he was shaking his head in utter disbelief. Then he began to crack up.

'You have got to be taking the mickey. You've been shagging "the unacceptable face of capitalism"? Christ almighty, the world really has gone mad . . . it's official!' Despite Rachel's obvious irritation, Fergus continued laughing.

'Look, I know what you think – about the prostitutes and the drugs and all that. But we've always really liked each other. We actually had a good thing at Cambridge, and I know you're going to laugh, but we kind of love each other. We have such fun when we're together . . . a lot more than I do with my dick of a husband.'

Fergus shared Rachel's view of her husband and always had done. He'd only met him a few times but Darren had lived up to every cliché in the book about dull accountants. Darren's idea of being reckless was putting two sugars in his coffee and the highlight of his week was the Neighbourhood Watch meeting. Fergus had long since concluded that Rachel had only married him because she'd felt her biological clock ticking and had sought out the security that a dependable man with a serious job could offer her.

'OK, OK, I believe you. So how did Darren find out about your, erm, dalliance? Text messages on the mobile phone?'

'No, this is the weird part. Colum and I had a lunch-time . . . rendezvous the other day at the Great Eastern. Now, on the way there I thought I was being followed and it turns out I was because someone took photographs of us meeting up. There are photos of me going into the hotel and there're a couple from outside of us in our room – before Colum closed the curtains – and ones of us kissing goodbye on the steps outside. Some bastard sent Darren the photos. He's always hated Colum and this was the last straw . . . I can't bear it. I've really, really fucked up. I can't bear what's happening to the children . . .' Rachel began sobbing again. She might have had major misgivings about her choice of husband but she had been willing to quash them for the sake of her children.

Fergus was about to speak when the front door bell rang. He excused himself, stood up and walked down the corridor. It was the postman. Fergus signed for an A4-sized envelope and came back to the table. As he tried to reassure Rachel, he absentmindedly opened the envelope. He pulled out the contents and stopped talking. Rachel knew immediately that something was up.

Fergus read the short note once, then again and finally a third time, his expression becoming darker and darker with each rereading. Visibly shaking, he handed Rachel the typed note and put his head in his hands. Rachel turned the letter round and read on. Within seconds she too was shaking.

FAO Fergus Callahan. I have irrefutable proof that you organised the bear raid that brought Geldlust down. I know who you did it with and I know exactly what you did – the roles of Alpha Max, Provincial Mutual, Rachel Maguire at the FSA, Steve Jones at Geldlust. I am not concerned about your actions but I will be handing over all the evidence I have accrued to the relevant authorities if £2 million is not deposited into a Swiss bank account by 25 December. I will be contacting you in four days' time to check up that you have made the relevant preparations. The details of the account are overleaf.'

Rachel's head fell into her hands and she began to cry.

Twenty-Two

Outside Colum's flat, Hoxton
Thursday, 16 December, 1.30 p.m.

Two things happened after Fergus phoned me about the blackmail letter he'd received and the photos that had been sent to Rachel's husband. First, I resigned myself to spending several years at Her Majesty's pleasure with an arsehole like the Blackwall Tunnel and a permanent case of cock breath. Second, it became abundantly clear who the rat in the group was. Everything had started going Pete Tong after Colum had been nicked. He had clearly been doing everything he could to save his fat neck and the three pockmarked chins it supported... cooperating on a certain level to show the authorities that he was a decent bloke who wanted to do the right thing and was merely surrounded by wrong 'uns. It could not be coincidence that John had got arrested merely hours after Colum's questioning, and the photos that Rachel's husband had been sent merely confirmed my suspicions, because only Colum had anything to gain from breaking up Darren and Rachel.

Frankly, I wasn't entirely surprised to hear about Rachel and Colum's dalliance. I knew that they'd had a damn good thing at university and I'd seen them flirting whenever they got wasted together, most notably after Bridget's funeral. I reckoned that Colum 'every hole's a goal' Boyd must have got bored with meaningless shags and sought something more fulfilling. Shit, I must have caught him on the way to Rachel's bedroom that last time down in Sussex when he'd unconvincingly claimed he was heading to the bathroom. Colum was a man who made sure he got whatever he wanted and he clearly wanted Rachel all to himself. He was also the kind of heartless shyster who wouldn't give a tinker's cuss about the effect her marriage break-up would have on her kids. He would have known the exact time Rachel was going to turn up to meet him at the Great Eastern and simply paid some private dick to stand outside and photograph her coming in and leaving with him. Shit, the devious mother-fucker had probably got them both to stand in the hotel room's window for a few seconds to get the necessary shots. After sending Darren the incriminating photos to ensure that they split up and that the path would be clear for him, he sent Fergus the blackmail letter.

At first I'd thought that the letter must have been sent by John, and that was who Fergus suspected too. Fergus agreed with me about Colum's sending Darren the photos but he argued that Colum wouldn't have bothered complicating things for 'a measly two mill'. He believed that John had lost it after taking too many drugs and argued that his relative impoverishment had made him want to increase his meagre winnings from Yogi. I felt that maybe Colum had sent the blackmail note to throw us off the scent. It was the kind of red herring a seasoned poker player like Colum would have thrown in the mix to ensure that he looked innocent. I figured that he must have concluded that his old victim John had tipped the FSA off to raid his firm and that he had then returned the favour by getting the police to raid John. For a while, I wasn't too sure if it was John or Colum who'd sent the blackmail letter, but I decided that Colum seemed the more likely candidate simply because he was the more immoral of the two. It was, without doubt, a bugger's muddle but one thing was for sure – it wasn't me, Fergus or Rachel who was up to no good.

It was these conclusions that explained why I found myself standing outside Colum's penthouse apartment on Thursday, nervously chain-smoking Marlboros waiting for the fat wanker to make an appearance. I'd been waiting there for over an hour when the devious bastard finally emerged. He looked pale and distraught, lighting up a cigarette even before he waddled on to the pavement.

He shuffled off down the street and I trailed him at a safe distance. I'd never followed anyone like this before and I soon found myself enjoying the experience. I felt as if I was in a James Bond film; it was exciting, and the power that I felt over my unsuspecting prey was exhilarating.

Occasionally, I would duck into a shop doorway for effect, although there was absolutely no reason to do so. Colum, seemingly lost in thought, never looked back, and even if he had he would almost certainly not have noticed me on a busy street twenty yards behind him. It just seemed like the right thing to do. It's what James would have done.

After about five minutes Colum arrived at a pub on a street corner called the Barley Mow that I'd been to several times with him. He took a cursory look around and went in. Good man, I thought, living up to all my preconceptions about how he'd be occupying himself during his enforced absence from work. No doubt after this lunchtime pint he'll be going off to bang some high-class slapper. I approached the pub, went down the side lane and peered through the window. It was your standard London hostelry – peculiar horse-related brass shit hanging on the walls, round wooden tables and regulars with cauliflower noses reading the newspaper at the bar. Colum was in the corner, supping a pint of lager and talking animatedly to some middle-aged bloke in a gabardine mac, a navy blue V-neck and straight black trousers. He had a thick moustache and his eyes were way too close together for my liking. This character was asking Colum questions and taking notes. He clearly found whatever Colum was saying fascinating. I immediately thought 'copper' and my shoulders slumped. I'd been hoping against hope that I was wrong, but things were beginning to stack up against Colum. He was clearly the grass . . . the rat in the pack.

After about half an hour of chit-chat with his new best friend Colum got up, shook hands and moved towards the exit on the other side of the pub from me. He left and started walking back in the direction of his flat. I turned my back on him as he passed by and felt confident that he hadn't glanced down the alleyway towards me. I didn't move. I wasn't interested in him any more.

After about two minutes Mr Moustache stood up, finished his pint, said goodbye to the barman and left. Again, I followed him at a safe distance. I had to know who this mystery feller was. As I followed him up Great Eastern Street, I prayed that it was some long-lost uncle Colum had been using to do some insider trading with. He was constantly making calls on his mobile. Unlike Colum, he seemed to have a suspicious nature. He kept on stopping at shop windows, pretending to look in; at one point I could have sworn he caught my eye. Despite this, I continued following him, my curiosity overcoming my fear. After a few more unconvincing glances into shop windows he turned into Shoreditch High Street. I felt nervous as I approached the corner of the road. If he'd noticed me then he could be waiting for me there. My pace slowed appreciably. My chest began to tighten and my heart rate went up a notch. I readied myself for a confrontation.

I turned the corner: he was nowhere to be seen. Fuck, I'd lost him. I upped my pace and walked down the road. Suddenly I saw him again. He was going up some steps into a faceless concrete building.

There was a blue lantern hanging outside and it had the word *Police* on it.

Now everything was clear. Without a second's thought I called up Fergus on the dodgy mobile and explained what I'd seen. His reply was predictably terse.

'The fat fuck!' Fergus's anger was evident. Not only was Colum potentially going to put us all in jail, he'd also screwed up Fergus's grand plan for a second bank job. 'That fucking fat fuck!' He spat the words out with contempt.

'Tell me about it. To think of all the years we've spent with that wanker! So, there really is no honour amongst thieves.'

After a few seconds of angry silence Fergus composed himself and spoke in his more traditional authoritative manner.

'Listen, I'm due to play squash with Colum this evening. He doesn't know we know about him squealing to the cops. We have the informational advantage. After I whup his fat ass, I'll get him high and quiz him back at mine . . . he always spills the beans when he's had a few lines of posh.'

We were both quite aware how indiscreet Colum could be after a couple of cheekies. Colum had told me and everyone else in the group when Fergus and Bridget were just getting together. They'd tried to keep it a secret for the first few weeks but Colum had bumped into them mid-embrace outside a cinema. Despite their pleas that he say nothing he had informed all the other members of the gang at a party later that night. Fergus had laughed it off at the time but I know that he'd have much preferred to inform the group himself.

'Yeah, but I want to strike while the iron is hot. I'm going to call him now and see if I can get anything out of him. I'm not sitting around like a lemon waiting for the cops to come and nick me. I tell you . . . if I think the radiks are about to get me I *will* do a runner.' I virtually shouted that last bit. I wanted Fergus to know that I meant every word – there was no way in hell I was going to merrily skip my way into a six by eight prison cell.

'OK, you quiz him, but be subtle. We can't let him know that we're on to him, OK?'

'Cool. Over and out, Fuckwit.'

'Laters, Skid Mark.'

I took a deep breath and then called Colum. I couldn't bear the fact that I had to make this call . . . that it had come to this.

'Yo, Cock Stick, how's it hanging?' Christ! What the fuck was I saying? I never used that retarded expression. It was the kind of crap a Wall Street banker might have said to a trader . . . probably followed by an enthusiastic high five. Colum was bound to see through my false bonhomie in about three nanoseconds. I'd just started the conversation and I was already hoofing it.

'All right, Skid Mark, it's hanging low and heavy as always. What's up?' He definitely sounded subdued. I suppose I would too if I'd just been forced to shop all my so-called mates. Still, if he had any suspicions he wasn't letting on.

'Well, I'm not working and your firm's temporarily shut down so we've got two choices: we can either sit at home stroking one out to internet porn or we can meet up and have a few pints and a game of pool. So whaddya reckon?'

'Sounds like a plan to me. See you in the Elbow Room in one hour.'

'Schweet! See you then, buddy.' I never, ever, used the word buddy. What was I doing? I was falling at the first hurdle. Surely he'd realise something was up . . .

The pool hall was full of huge, tattooed, bearded monsters . . . and the men weren't much better. Much to my irritation Colum was on fire. The lardy cocksucker was taking me right back to school. As a rule, I'd have been giving him a lesson on the pool table but understandably I was edgy and tense and my game was suffering. He was 4–0 up and I hadn't come close to potting the black once. A fucking window-licker on PCP would have been ripping me apart, such was my nervy, stuttering play. My atrocious form was such a major preoccupation that I'd temporarily forgotten that one of my oldest mates was in the process of betraying me.

The conversation had been serious and guarded initially. There wasn't much to laugh about. Colum had described in detail the FSA raid and explained, without any prompting from me, that he hadn't said a word to 'those little pricks' about Yogi. He promised me that he'd left no incriminating evidence and that he, and therefore we, would get away with it. It was during the fifth game that I decided to up the ante and start getting some answers.

'What about John? Do you think he'll talk, if pushed?'

'Mate, I have my worries – I don't know, but what I do know is that Richard is doing everything he can to make both him and me talk. It's quite obvious that the greasy butt plug doesn't have any solid evidence, which is why he's trying to play us all off against each other. We'd have heard from the pigs by now if they had anything concrete.' Colum slammed another ball in with a flourish and grinned at me. The stress of recent events didn't seem to be getting to him at all. He'd once told me that 'pressure makes diamonds' and, unfortunately, when it came to pool it seemed he wasn't lying.

'Just a goddamn minute, mate. Richard knew all about what I used to get up to at the Black Cat so someone in our group is *definitely* talking.' I watched Colum pot another ball. This was becoming genuinely embarrassing.

'That is weird . . . and it makes no sense to me. Whoever told Richard about your whoremongering is trying to hurt you plain and simple. They probably know that you couldn't give a fuck about losing your job . . . but they also know about the awful embarrassment you'll feel when your poor parents find out they've got a degenerate sex pest for a son!' Colum sliced the black perfectly into the centre pocket, as if to emphasise his little dig. I couldn't believe the whipping I was getting but did my best to pretend that I didn't feel as though I was on the verge of a nervous breakdown.

'Easy, tiger. Pots and kettles, stones and glass houses and all that,' I said as I collected the balls and began racking them up. I was aware that I was being too defensive and I really wanted to keep a cool head. I had to remember that it was me doing the interrogation, not him.

'Yeah, but, mate, I've never pretended to be anything other than what I am. But you've always given it this righteous, virtuous horseshit and now it's coming back to bite you on the arse. You and Fergus think your shit don't stink but here's news for you both: it does.' Colum took a gulp of his pint and stared at me defiantly. I had come here expecting to give him a hard time but it seemed to be me who was on the receiving end. I took a deep breath and tried to divert the conversation away from my failings.

'What do you mean about Fergus? Of all of us, he's the least bad.'

'Yeah, maybe. But look at him and Bridget. They weren't perfect by any means, mate. I've had her crying on my shoulder telling me what a brute the man can be. I think he might have hit her a couple of times . . . and I don't fucking believe they were engaged. If anything, those two were in trouble towards the end.' This was genuinely surprising and I didn't believe a word of it. Bridget had never told me anything about this. It was obviously just Colum shit-stirring again.

'Fuck off, mate. They had a damn good thing and you know they did. I suppose you'll be telling next me that

Rachel isn't just a bit of fun for you . . . a MILF you can pork for a bit of variety after all those high-class hookers?' I replied, thinking attack was the best form of defence here.

Colum's face went puce and he strode up to me with a menacing purpose in his step. He was gripping the pool cue in his right hand as if he were about to smash it around my head. He was baring his teeth and had fury in his eyes. I'd never seen the man look so angry. I took a step back and readied myself for a serious kicking. Colum put his face right up to mine and started spitting words out whilst jabbing his chubby finger into my chest. I could see a few people behind him staring at what looked likely to be a proper rumble.

'Listen, mate. Don't you dare talk about Rachel like that. You have no *fucking* idea about me and her, *all right*? I don't give *two* shits what you think. We've always had a good thing and we still *do*. Don't you dare fucking judge me or her, OK?' Each sentence was accompanied by a sharp jab in the chest. Colum's eyes looked deranged. I had most definitely pissed on his strawberries. I tried my best to show him and our growing audience that I wasn't shitting bricks.

'OK, mate. Take it easy. I'm sorry.' I took a deep breath and regained my composure. Colum seemed to calm down as quickly as he'd got angry. I decided then that it was time to get him on the ropes, show him that I knew what was going on. I'd been spending too long on the back foot; now it was his turn.

'If that's the way you feel I suppose it's understandable that you sent her husband those photos.'

'Yeah, I bet that's what you think. You and fucking Fergus working it all out, yeah? Well, it's bullshit. I would never do something like that. Force her to split up? Hurt her kids? No, mate, you and Fergus have got me mistaken for a right cunt and I ain't that.'

Colum's bullshit was exceptional. He made Richard look like a rank amateur. He had spoken with just the right mix of anger and hurt. Christ, he was so believable he almost took me in for a second. After a pause I thought I'd try a different tack.

'So, is that what you've been trying to tell me? You almost said something in the bog after Bridget's funeral and again at your gaff in Sussex. Was that it?'

There was a long pause. Colum looked at me. It was clear he was trying to decide whether or not to tell me. After a few seconds his shoulders slumped and he said: 'Yes, mate. I was just going to tell you about me and Rachel, that's all.' But I knew immediately that wasn't what it had been about. Whilst I wasn't entirely convinced that the rest of his story was bullshit, this most definitely was. Indeed, his inability to lie convincingly here made me feel that maybe he might even have been telling the truth before. Still, there was no point pushing it. I decided to try some horse crap of my own.

'What about Fergus, then? Maybe he's doing all this?'

'Why?'

'I don't fucking know. Maybe he's lost it after Bridge? Gone all leftie?'

'Doesn't make any sense. He's got the most to lose . . . this has fucked up his baby, Operation Grizzly. He's put shitloads of work into that and I know he's seriously gutted. No, I'm afraid if it's anyone in the group, it's more likely to be you,' said Colum, staring me straight in the eyes.

I really hadn't been expecting that. I suppose innocent people are wrongly accused all the time, but this took my breath away. I stared at Colum for a few seconds and then realised that it was the classic behaviour of an accused party. Of course. If I were guilty then I'd try to turn the tables too. When I'd got over the initial shock I spoke up.

'Yeah, mate, that's right. I've got some big agenda against all my old mates and for some sick reason am doing my best to fuck 'em up and scupper my chances of making serious cash out of Yogi in the process. Pull the other one, it's got fucking bells on!' I'd mustered enough righteous anger to convince him he was barking up the wrong tree.

'Well, it could be you . . . but if you want to know what I *really* think I'll tell you. This is almost certainly John and Richard. You've noticed John hasn't lost his job, and when I asked him he seemed to think he's not going to. Richard knows about the drugs bust and he wants to get us all done to get back at us for the way we treated him. He can get John fired at the drop of a hat and undoubtedly would have done so unless John's helping him with his enquiries. The only one he's got any leverage over is John and he's using his power over him to get to us all. I also reckon it's Richard who tipped off the FSA about me. It's the only scenario that makes sense.'

Suddenly, everything wasn't as clear cut as it had been ten minutes before. Colum was talking a lot of sense. Richard hated us all and John knew about everything that had so far been used against us. Richard must have threatened John and then used the information John had given him to get to us all. Meanwhile, John, realising that he wasn't going to get any money from Colum's fund because of the FSA raid, had decided to up his measly winnings by blackmailing Fergus. I suddenly felt queasy. I knew the colour was draining from my face. I walked away from Colum without saying a word and stumbled to the toilet in the corner. Once inside I had to steady myself against a wall. After a few seconds I staggered into a cubicle and lowered myself on to the bowl. I closed my eyes and held my head in my hands. Maybe Colum really had worked it out. Maybe good old John was the rat. I started feeling dizzy. My brain was buzzing with too many thoughts. I felt claustrophobic in the cubicle. My heart rate was rising and I could feel droplets of sweat running down my forehead. My breathing had become fast and shallow. I was clearly having some sort of panic attack. I forced myself to take long, deep breaths and felt my heart rate slowly return to normal. After a few minutes I began to calm down. I went out and splashed some cold water on my face. When I looked into the mirror I saw a pale, ghostly figure staring back at me. After a few more splashes I decided that I'd pull out the big guns when I returned. I'd tell Colum that I knew about his meeting with the copper. I spent another minute preparing my spiel and walked back to our table.

Colum wasn't there.

Twenty-Three

Fitness First gym, Spitalfields
Thursday, 16 December, 7.30 p.m.

A s with every squash game, a post-match analysis took place in the showers, and, as always, it was Fergus who led the discussion. As the two men washed themselves in their adjoining cubicles Fergus held forth. His condescending manner irritated Colum deeply. Both guys were dangerously competitive and every one of Fergus's victories piqued Colum's vast, pulsating ego.

'Mate, you could have had me in the second game, if you'd been faster around the court. I'm sorry, Colum, but until you lose your jelly belly you're not going anywhere. You'll also notice that, once again, the more games we played the fewer points you won. You might even be a more skilful player than me but your fitness is dire. Lay off the cigarettes, lose a couple of stone and then maybe we'll have a proper game.' Fergus was laying it on even thicker than usual. He'd always enjoyed revelling in a post-match triumph but today he really was doing his damnedest to needle Colum.

'Whatever, mate. I'm coming to get you and you're running scared. It's a question of when, not if, I beat you,' said a still red-faced Colum, fully aware that Fergus had a valid point.

'You keep telling yourself that and you might believe it one day. Get a grip, man! Your ego's writing cheques your body can't cash!' laughed Fergus.

Although the conversation seemed superficially aggressive to the other guys in the changing room Colum and Fergus had been exchanging similar banter for about fifteen years. They'd first played at Cambridge and had managed a match at least once a week ever since. In the absence of any genuine connection it was a pleasant routine that helped create a temporary bond between the two. It was a classic way for two alpha males to spend time with each other. Colum always used to beat Fergus but as he'd got fatter and more sluggish the balance had tipped in Fergus's favour – much to Colum's dismay. It was the only exercise Colum ever did, and on this occasion the fourth game had proved too much. Colum had looked as though he was about to have a coronary and Fergus had been a little worried. Colum's face had turned bright red and he'd begun wheezing like an asthmatic with emphysema. Age and his debilitating lifestyle were clearly catching up with him, and despite his protestations Fergus had insisted that they finish the game there and then. As he'd said somewhat melodramatically, he couldn't handle two friends dying within a month of each other.

After drying off and getting dressed the two old sparring partners headed back to Fergus's nearby flat. Much to Colum's surprise, Fergus informed him on the walk that he had a gram of star-quality Bolivian flake back at his. Fergus usually only got wired on special occasions, but Colum's vast appetite for nose candy ensured that he didn't question this turn-up for the books. He simply relished the thought of getting high. Meanwhile Fergus relished the thought of Colum's likely indiscretion once he'd got high.

As soon as they were back at the flat, Fergus pulled out the wrap of coke and handed it to Colum, whose lower abdomen was already experiencing the gurgling that always preceded the inevitable disco plops. Whilst Fergus was in the kitchen retrieving a couple of bottles of Becks from the fridge Colum went about his racking-up duties diligently and professionally, making sure that his line was just a smidgen bigger than Fergus's as any good drug addict would. He snorted it with a theatrical flourish and after a few seconds felt the familiar rush of euphoria envelop him. He sat back in the armchair with a contented smile on his face, the loss on the squash court a fading memory.

Once Fergus was back and had snorted his line they began chatting away. Colum told Fergus his theory about John's treachery and Fergus pretended to agree – he knew who the real culprit was. Then they got on to the subject of

Bridget's death and things took an interesting turn. It became obvious that something was troubling Colum and Fergus began doing everything in his power to prise it out of him. If Colum hadn't been buzzing he might have discerned Fergus's agenda but his exploding dopamines were preventing him from picking up on it.

'I'm still really unsure about what happened. I mean, Bridget just wasn't the sort of girl to kill herself . . . even if she was high . . . even if she had lost her job. I think there's something more to it, don't you?' Fergus said, staring intently into Colum's glassy eyes . . . willing him to speak.

'Well, yeah, maybe . . . erm, I don't know, mate. It doesn't seem right, but then I suppose it never does.' Colum's teeth were gnashing away as he racked up another fattie. Fergus noticed that the other man's hand was shaking slightly. It could have been the Charlie.

'She did seem a little confused towards the end. She was talking about some bloke in a scarf following her, but as far as I know she never found out who he was. You don't think . . . you don't think that maybe she was pushed?' Fergus probed, edging closer to Colum.

Colum looked up with a start. He couldn't disguise the shock on his face. Fergus had touched a nerve here, and what's more Colum knew that his face had betrayed the fact that he had.

'Mate, I don't think so,' he stuttered. 'I mean what the fuck? No! We . . . we just have to accept that she fell to her death.'

Fergus's eyes narrowed. ' "She fell to her death" . . . don't you mean she killed herself?'

'No . . . not necessarily. She might have fallen by accident. Anyway, what makes you think she was confused?' said Colum, desperately trying to change the subject.

'Oh, I don't know. She wasn't quite her usual self towards the end. I felt something was going on.' Fergus took a long, deep breath. 'Look, what I'm about to ask you may sound strange, but it's been playing on my mind. It's to go no further, right?'

'Right,' said Colum, praying that they were moving off the subject of Bridget's death.

'OK.' Fergus took another deep breath. 'Do you think Steve was trying to get back together with Bridget? I know very well that he regrets how it ended all those years ago. Christ, he's only had one proper bird since Bridge and before she and I got together he told me a few times that he was still in love with her. And I saw the way he looked at her right up until the end. I'm just wondering if he was making a play for her.' Fergus was speaking in a very measured tone, as if he had been preparing to ask this question for some time. As he finished speaking he pointed at the wrap of Charlie, signalling that Colum should rack up another couple of lines. Colum didn't need to be asked twice and set about his duty, crushing up a bit more coke with his credit card as he replied.

'Whoa, mate, hold your horses. Steve may be many things but he isn't that kind of bloke. No, I chatted with Bridget a lot towards the end and she never mentioned anything like that.'

'What do you mean, you "chatted with Bridget a lot towards the end"? What the fuck does that mean?' said Fergus, glaring at Colum, his veiled accusation sounding increasingly aggressive.

'Oh, come on, mate? Don't be ridiculous! Christ, even if I'd wanted to, do you think she'd have given it a second's thought? And anyway I didn't want to . . .' It was Colum's turn to take a deep breath. He paused for an unnaturally long time and then said it, the words Fergus had been waiting for: 'But there is something I've been meaning to tell you. Something I've been wanting to tell you for weeks but couldn't bring myself to . . .'

Fergus leant forward, a look of total concentration on his face 'Go on . . .'

Two hours later Fergus led Colum to his front door. He opened it and looked out at the street. It was coming up to 11.30 and there was no one around. Colum shuffled past him with his gym bag over his shoulder and stopped in the doorway. Fergus smiled at his old pal.

'Mate, I'm really pleased you told me. I can see why it must have been really hard keeping it to yourself and I completely understand why you didn't mention it before. I really appreciate your honesty. You're a true friend.'

'No worries, mate. Thanks for being understanding. You know what? It's a lovely night and I'm buzzing . . . I think

I'm gonna walk home. See you later.'

They gave each other an awkward coked-up hug and Colum waddled off down the street.

Fergus closed the door and walked back into his living room.

Twenty-Four

Steve's flat, Old Street
Thursday, 16 December, 11.50 p.m.

I WAS LYING ON MY sofa trying to analyse this increasingly complicated situation. I assessed all the evidence in as logical a fashion as possible, occasionally sitting up and writing down some of the more salient points. Slowly but surely, I was piecing together the jigsaw. I knew that the answer was there somewhere but I'd been struggling to find it for over an hour.

It seemed to me that there were three main possibilities: John was the rat, Colum was the rat or they were both rats. I could hardly bring myself to believe that good old John was behind this shit storm. He was just too nice a bloke. But then I started thinking about him and how much he'd changed since Cambridge. Who really knew what was going on in that freak's head now? By all accounts, he'd been caning the drugs of late and he'd stalked Bridget just before she died. He was also relatively poor compared to the rest of us and had made the least out of Yogi – a mere hundred and twenty grand and probably nothing more if, as seemed likely, the FSA had their way with Colum's fund. He was also full of anger and jealousy – particularly towards Colum who was noticeably the first to come a cropper. Was it a coincidence that Colum got a visit from the FSA after another weekend of victimising poor John? And Colum was right when he said that Richard had leverage over John having found out about the drugs bust. Who else was feeding Richard this info if not John, fearful that he'd lose his job? More important, why had John still not been fired? I'd called John up to ask him what Richard was up to several times during the day but his phone was off. Arguably, his silence spoke volumes.

Colum, on the other hand, was an unashamed beast of a man. He was a greedy, ruthless degenerate who was capable of disgraceful behaviour if it furthered his own ambitions. Surely, only someone with his deeply compromised personality would be willing to perpetrate the unpleasantness that had befallen us all. The evidence was pretty compelling: John was nicked soon after Colum had had his run-in with the rozzers and no one other than Colum would have had any interest in splitting up Rachel and Darren. He also knew all about my relationship with Frankfurt's finest bordello and I had seen with my own eyes that he'd been talking to the pigs. Sending Fergus that blackmail note was just the kind of sly manoeuvre that cunning bastard would have employed to throw us off the scent. Colum also smoked, unlike John, which meant that he could have been the fucker trying to freak me out at two in the morning. No, on balance, it had to be Colum. All the evidence pointed his way. He'd got nicked and Richard was threatening him – so he was doing everything in his power to protect his flabby arse whilst feeding Richard information that would turn the heat towards us. It had to be Colum.

I'd just reached this conclusion when the phone rang. Talk of the devil and he's sure to give you a bell.

'Hi, Skid Mark. It's Cock Stick.'

'All right mate, to what do I owe this pleasure? Where are you?' I tried to sound as relaxed as possible. I wanted him to believe that we were still old pals who'd just been out for a game of pool, nothing more.

'Well, I'm just getting home now and there's something I want to tell you. It's something I've been wanting to tell you and Fergus ever since Bridget died.' He was obviously buzzing. His nasal tones and throaty voice suggested he'd hoofed a fair amount of bugle and smoked a couple of hundred Marlboro reds to boot.

'Yeah, and what's that?' I said, steadying myself for another torrent of misinformation.

'Well, listen . . .' Suddenly there was a scream and then a cracking sound as if he'd dropped the phone, followed by some dull, muffled noises. It sounded as though Colum was being hit. I could hear thuds and whimpers. I began shouting 'Colum' but there was no response. I grabbed my coat and, with the phone still pressed to my ear, ran out of the house.

Colum's flat was only an eight-minute walk away. If I ran, I'd be there in four. As I sprinted towards Hoxton Square I suddenly thought I heard a faint voice down the line. I stopped dead in my tracks. My own heavy breathing made listening difficult. I shouted, 'Mate . . . mate, are you there?' my voice high-pitched and strained.

'Help me . . . help me.' That was all I heard. It was barely discernible. It sounded like Colum but it was more of a whisper than anything else. I started sprinting faster than before, my heart racing away. By the time I'd arrived in Hoxton Square the sweat was pouring down my back.

As soon as I turned the corner into the square I saw him. He was lying facedown in the middle of the road twenty steps from his front door. A streetlight directly above him lit his body up as if he were a corpse on a stage. My stomach turned to water. I was panting like a lunatic. The sweat streamed down my face as I slowed down and approached the body. As I got nearer I could see a pool of dark blood gathering around his head. I shouted his name once, then again. No response. I got on my hands and knees and shook him gently. Nothing. I tried to roll him on to his back. It took some effort but after a few seconds I managed it, and immediately regretted it. His eyes rolled back in his head. He was pale and there was a deep gash on his forehead, and his hair was matted with thick, brown blood. I gently placed his head on my knees and prayed that he was OK. I pulled his head towards me and put my ear to his mouth. There was nothing. I put my finger to his neck. Nothing.

I sat there spotlit by the streetlight on the quiet, empty street with my dead friend cradled in my lap. I dropped my head and started sobbing uncontrollably. For all his faults Colum had been my mate. For all I knew he might have been innocent of all my accusations. The tears rolled down my face. Why was this happening to us?

Suddenly, a car screamed round the corner. It screeched to a halt just feet away and three uniformed police officers piled out and surrounded me. One of them held a pistol aimed directly at my head. The other two had pulled out and extended their retractable batons. All three seemed to shout in unison: 'Get down on the fucking ground NOW! Lie face down in the fucking road NOW!' I didn't need to be asked twice. I gently lowered Colum's head on to the tarmac and did as they said. Within a second one of the officers had his knee in my back and had pulled my hands up behind me. After another second I felt one and then the other wrist placed in a stiff set of handcuffs.

The tears were still streaming down my face.

Twenty-Five

Bishopsgate Police Station
Friday, 17 December, 8.15 a.m.

'So, LET'S GO THROUGH THIS again. You were called by Mr Boyd at approximately midnight. He was just talking to you when you heard him being attacked. You ran over to him in about five or so minutes and discovered his body just seconds before the police arrived? Is that about the size of it?' asked Sergeant David Miller . . . the very officer I'd had a cup of tea with just weeks before. I'd been dealing with some other wankers immediately upon my arrival at the police station but I'd explained my connection to Miller and so after a restless five hours during which I lay on a thin rubber mattress inhaling detergent fumes in one of their puke-stained holding cells they'd called him up and persuaded him to come in early.

The seven hours before Miller had arrived had been deeply unpleasant. I'd literally been 'caught red-handed' and the cops who had accompanied me in the car back to the station had made it clear that I was most definitely going down. As I sat there trembling with sweaty fear the grinning bastard in the front passenger seat had turned round, shaken his head and declared that it was an 'open and shut case'. Even in my confused and desperate state I realised that things didn't look good for me. I had been found sweat-soaked, panting and covered in blood with a newly dead body in my arms and no one else within fifty yards of me. As the realisation that I was the prime suspect for Colum's murder sank in I began to feel nauseous. At one point I thought that the cop next to me was going to be wiping my dinner off his lap before the journey was over. I was still trying to come to terms with the death of my friend but a major new priority was rearing its ugly head – avoiding becoming a permanent resident at Wormwood Scrubs. I desperately wanted to tell them how unjust their accusations were but my wide-eyed, stuttering protestations of inno-cence would have made even my most loyal friends doubt me . . . in the hypothetical situation that I still had any. The realisation that I was facing this ordeal alone made it all the more alarming. I wished Bridge had been there to set them straight. I wished she'd been there to comfort me. I just wished she'd been there. Still, I had to be strong. I had to right this wrong, and ten minutes after arriving at the station I'd thought of something that might help convince my accusers that I was a wronged man. I reiterated my defence to Miller.

'That is exactly the size of it. Look at my mobile and his mobile and you'll see that I'm telling the truth,' I told him desperately. The sergeant stared at me with his unblinking eyes. I tried to return his unflinching glare but couldn't. My eyes began to moisten. I blinked and then blinked again. I looked down, hoping he wouldn't take my weakness as a sign of guilt. As I stared at the floor I longed again to have Bridge at my side. I longed to feel her hand in mine. After a few more seconds of tense silence Miller spoke up. His voice was stern and authoritative. He had ditched the conciliatory manner of our last encounter.

'Yes, we have done that and the calling records do concur with your story. It's clear that you, aka Skid Mark, were called by Mr Boyd, aka Cock Stick. It seems that you were over a kilometre away when he called. Significantly, neither phone had been turned off by the time our officers reached you.' This was news to me. My phone had been confiscated immediately after I'd been handcuffed. I felt a wave of relief envelop me as I realised that this made my story even more credible.

'We can also divulge that Mr Boyd's wallet is missing and seeing as it isn't on you and it wasn't in the vicinity of his body, nor at his flat, we can only assume that this was a mugging. We have also spoken to two witnesses who saw a man wearing a scarf and a woolly hat running away from the scene of the crime just before you arrived. Unfortunately, neither saw his face but it obviously wasn't you. It appears Mr Boyd was attacked from behind and that when he fell forward he smashed his head on the tarmac . . . which is almost certainly the cause of death as no weapon appears to have been used.'

I knew that the evidence now indicated that I was an innocent man. I felt my hunched shoulders droop and my heart rate begin to normalise. I willed out the next words Miller uttered: 'Anyway, you'll be pleased to hear that after a few more questions you'll be free to leave . . . though we may well call you in for questioning again. You're not to leave London until we say you can.'

I couldn't disguise my relief. I let out a huge sigh – a breath I'd been holding in for what seemed like hours. Poor Colum had simply been the unfortunate victim of a violent mugging that had gone horribly wrong. A particularly unpleasant part of me felt that some form of poetic justice had been meted out . . . he was after all the treacherous rat in the pack. His testimony against the rest of us had died with him . . . and perhaps his death meant the rest of the gang would now be safe. However, our salvation had come at a high price, for now there was no chance whatsoever that we'd get our hands on any of the millions Colum's fund had accrued from Yogi. That gentlemen's agreement had died with him on the tarmac of Hoxton Square. I tried to dismiss these callous thoughts from my mind. I had just lost a friend whom I'd known for almost two decades. He might have been a rude, inconsiderate prick but he was our rude, inconsiderate prick. Despite his constant need to break taboos, there had always been a line that he had chosen not to cross with me.

After another few seconds, Sergeant Miller asked the other copper to leave the room and sat down across the table from me. He turned off the machine that had been recording my statement and leant towards me conspiratorially. I leant in closer to hear his words.

'Look, Steve, there're a couple of things I'm going to disclose regarding the death of your girlfriend Bridget. I'm telling you this because we're going nowhere in this case and, so far, you've been cooperating with us fully. But what I'm about to do is not . . . well, let's just say I haven't cleared it with my superiors. Do you still want to hear it?' I suspect Miller knew that there was no need to ask that question. I had to have answers. I had to understand why everything was falling apart.

'Absolutely. What is it? What's going on?' I suddenly felt that if I could get closer to the truth about Bridget's death maybe the confusion and the madness of the last few weeks would begin to make sense.

'OK, there're two things you need to know about that Monday morning at the Barbican. First of all . . .' Miller took a deep breath, 'there was someone else in the room when Bridget died. A witness in the building opposite who heard the screams when Bridget fell saw a figure leave the room just after she fell. This witness was a drug user who initially didn't want to get involved with the police but her conscience got the better of her last week. We've got no description of the person who left . . . but we are now viewing this as a likely murder enquiry, though we haven't officially changed its status yet.'

My mouth dropped. I could feel my eyes widen with shock. Was this really happening? Just when I'd thought that things couldn't get worse, they had. My head rolled forward and I put it in my hands. Who the hell would want to murder Bridge? Eventually I looked up. Sergeant Miller was staring at me. I felt a tear drip down my cheek.

'What the fuck? She was murdered?' I still couldn't grasp this new information. I was hoping for clarity but all I was getting was more questions.

'It looks that way. And there's more.' Miller took another deep breath and continued: 'As you know, we took all your gang's fingerprints and DNA. Well . . . they were all there, some older than others. But there was one other set of finger-prints there too. A set that was fresher than the rest of them . . . a set that we found on the glass table over some of the other ones. Whoever this guy is, he's got no record but he was definitely there in the last twenty-four hours of Bridget's life. If we catch this chap we might just have Bridget's killer.'

Miller sat back and folded his arms. He said nothing, to allow me to take in this second bombshell. I was totally stunned. After a few seconds I heard myself say: 'Christ! Have you got any leads . . . any thoughts?' My mind was racing away, trying to remember if Bridget knew anyone else who might have visited her during her final day on this planet.

'Lots, but none that lead anywhere. That's why I'm talking to you. Have *you* got any thoughts?' Miller said, pointing at me with his bony finger.

'No. I'm sorry. I can't think of anyone else Bridget hung out with. We were her best mates.'

There was a long pause. Eventually, Miller spoke up: 'OK. Well, look – you're free to go now. Keep my card and ring me if you think of anything, no matter how small, and remember this conversation didn't happen, OK?'

With that he stood up and beckoned me towards the door. I retrieved my phone, keys, wallet and shoelaces from the officer behind the desk and walked out of the police station into a crisp December morning.

I'd go home, have a shower and then confront him.

Twenty-Six

John's flat, Camden
Saturday, 18 December, 11.15 a.m.

I KNOCKED ON JOHN'S DOOR. I hadn't bothered to phone him because he wasn't taking any calls. After a few minutes I heard his shuffling footsteps in the corridor. Eventually, he called out, 'Hello, who is it?' His words were tentative. There was fear in his voice.

'It's me, Steve. Open up.' After another long pause I heard him slide the chain across and twist the door handle. He stood there pale and skinny in his boxer shorts and vest. It looked as if I'd woken him up. He reluctantly beckoned me in and I strolled past him. Once in his lounge, I turned round and said my piece.

'OK, John, enough bullshit. Everything's got out of fucking control . . . I've got some questions and you'd better give me some fucking answers right now.'

John just stood there like a statue, glaring at me. He'd

obviously been on the gear until the early hours. He might not have slept at all. I had decided on the way over not to inform him about Colum's death. I didn't want to complicate the situation and couldn't bear the thought that he might actually be pleased that his old nemesis had been killed.

'OK, so here's the deal. Fergus and I are convinced you're the rat in the pack and unless you can prove otherwise things are going to get pretty nasty for you, OK?' We weren't really convinced of this at all. In fact, both of us were kind of satisfied that it had been Colum who'd been spilling the beans. Still, I'd agreed with Fergus on the phone that I'd go and scare John a bit and find out if he'd been saying anything he shouldn't. Despite Colum's death there was still a chance we could be implicated in Geldlust's demise, and if John had told the police anything to protect his bony arse then we needed to know about it. I also wanted answers about those last hours of Bridget's life and I felt sure John had some. I continued: 'We know that Richard's blackmailing you into grassing us up. We know that he knows about the drugs bust and that he's the sort of nasty prick who'd tell your boss about it just to piss you off . . . so, tell me how come you've still got your job?'

John stared at me. After a suitably lengthy pause he began speaking. His voice was quiet and subdued. 'OK, he did threaten me, but I haven't said anything to him, I swear. He's told me that if I don't tell on you guys by this Wednesday he'll inform my firm . . . but I don't care. I'm not going to tell him anything and if I get fired then that's the way it goes.' He crossed his arms defiantly to emphasise his point.

'That's very big of you . . . taking one for the team and all that. Not sure I believe you, though. But I'll let that go. Next question. I know you were around Bridget's when she died – a witness has identified you and your fingerprints are all over her stuff.' This was a bluff but I thought it might just work if he wasn't on the ball. John was very clever but he wasn't street smart.

'I wasn't there when she jumped,' he blurted out. He said it way too quickly. That was weird.

'Mate, we know you were around hers that weekend, so tell me what really happened or things really will get nasty. I might have to be telling Fergus about you going round there and selling her drugs . . .' There was a clear implied threat in my last statement. Despite John's supposed karate expertise, if it came to a fight between those two the smart money was on the gnarly Scottish feller.

'OK, OK . . . I'll admit I went round there that weekend but it was on Saturday morning at about eleven o'clock. I sold her a whole bunch of drugs, did a couple of lines with her and went on my way. I swear I never went back there. I promise.' His eyes told me he was telling the truth. He never had been a great liar . . . unless he'd learnt recently.

'So, it was you who sold her the drugs that weekend? Yeah, I thought it probably was and I reckon Fergus does too . . . You know he's not going to be best pleased when he hears that, don't you?'

'Yeah . . . please don't tell him. There's no point. Please.' There was genuine worry in John's voice – a bit pathetic really, considering he was supposed to be the karate expert.

'OK, OK, I won't. So, if it wasn't you seen in the room just after Bridget fell then who the fuck was it?'

'I don't know . . . but if I was a betting man I'd say it was probably Rachel.' What the fuck? He had to be joking. He was clutching at straws now . . . surely just trying to deflect attention away from himself.

'What . . . so Rachel killed Bridget is your theory, is it?'

'You don't know Rachel at all, do you? She's a real bunny boiler. Her problems with Darren are all because she's a jealous headcase. For God's sake, she's been having anger management therapy for over a decade. I'm telling you, she is one sick lady . . . and she's always been jealous of Bridget. She even blames Bridget for her losing her job at Geldlust . . . She's delusional. If I were you I'd be questioning her.' John was jabbing his finger at me, trying to intimidate me with his convoluted horseshit.

'Mate, you've lost it. You must think I was born yesterday. I'm not standing around listening to this crap . . . and don't you fucking dare open your mouth about Yogi, OK?'

'Don't worry, I won't. I've got as much to lose as you do.'

I walked out without saying goodbye. I hadn't gained much info from John but I'd left his grubby flat a little more convinced that it was Colum, and not John, who had been the rat. I walked along a rubbish-strewn street towards the tube station unsure what to do. I was surrounded by devious wankers intent on shafting me. I didn't know who I could trust any more. There was no one. The gang was no more.

It was after a few minutes of solitary ambling that I saw a reflection in a corner shop window. Someone was following me.

Someone dressed in a hat and scarf.

I continued walking down the road as if nothing were wrong. Every now and again I'd check a shop window as I passed to see if I was still being followed. I was . . . it was real. It was clearly a man and it obviously wasn't John, so who the fuck was it? A copper? After nonchalantly strolling along for another few blocks I formed a plan. It was time to turn the tables. I needed to find out who this guy was and what the fuck he was up to.

At the next crossroads I turned left and immediately sprinted to the other side of the road. I squeezed between two parked cars and then crouched down and waited for my stalker to appear, my heart racing. Sure enough, after about five seconds he turned the corner. He wore a long navy blue overcoat and walked with a definite purpose to his stride. Although he wore his scarf bunched about around his chin and had pulled his baseball cap low down on his head there was something familiar about him. When he realised he couldn't see me he stopped dead in his tracks and scanned the whole street. Fortunately for me there were lanes leading off to the left and right only about twenty yards down the road. It was conceivable that I'd gone down either one. He broke into a light jog and arrived at the next crossroads. He looked down both ways, paused, and then headed left. I took off and followed him to the corner. As I did so, I removed my hat and turned my overcoat inside out; it had a dark green lining and would look quite different if he happened to glance back. I followed at a safe distance and tried to position other pedestrians between me and him. I smirked to myself – the hunter had now become the hunted.

After about five minutes my stalker gave up and entered a pub. He looked around as he pushed through the door but didn't catch a glimpse of me. I approached the entrance carefully and looked through a small glass section in the door. I could see the figure with his back to me ordering a drink at the bar. He took it to a table by the opposite window and slowly removed the scarf and then the hat. I couldn't believe my eyes. It was Richard fucking Stimp.

Richard took out a small pocket diary and began writing notes in it. Every now and again he took a little sip from his half pint. He was engrossed. Again, I enjoyed the sensation of spying on someone. As I did so, a plan formed in my brain. All I had to do was wait and make sure I wasn't seen. I found a window with a single transparent pane and stood there in the cold chain-smoking cigarettes.

After about fifteen minutes, Richard got up and headed to the toilet. Much to my annoyance he took his notebook with him. Still, he'd left what I was really after. As soon as he'd disappeared I marched into the pub and straight up to his table. I pulled the sleeve of my jumper over my hand and grabbed his glass by its top. I then placed it in my inside pocket and hightailed it out of there before anyone could ask me any awkward questions. Once outside I hailed a black cab.

I opened the door, sat down and said, 'Bishopsgate police station.'

On the journey over I pulled out Sergeant Miller's card and called him. I asked him to meet me at the police station, saying it would be very much in his interest. He was already there when I arrived, an expectant expression plastered all over his face. I gingerly handed over the glass and told him to see if the prints on it were the same as the unknown ones that had been found at Bridget's flat. He asked me whose they were and I said that I wouldn't tell him unless they came up trumps. After fifteen minutes he returned. His expression gave nothing away. Then he broke out into a big smile and confirmed that they were the missing fingerprints.

Suddenly, everything clicked into place. I'd been such a fool. It was all so bleeding obvious now. How could I have not seen the truth when it had been staring me in the face all along? That scumbag Richard had always fancied Bridget. He must have gone round to her flat and started professing his undying love for her after Geldlust had fired her and she'd blamed him. She would have been totally boxed and almost certainly would have laughed him off the stage. The poor fool's fragile ego wouldn't have been able to deal with the rejection and, in a fit of fury, he must have pushed her out of the window. After that he'd properly lost it – even more so after we pulled a number on the bank that he and his dad worked at. That fetid piece of dick cheese had conspired against us all from the very beginning, using his power over John to get all the information he needed to hurt us. Our constant mockery over the years had sent him fucking crazy and the little piece of shit wanted revenge, pure and simple. He'd made it his dedicated mission to fuck us all up and he had almost succeeded. But there was no way in hell I was going to let that slimy squit succeed. He'd rue the fucking day that we— my thought process was suddenly disturbed by Sergeant Miller.

'So, tell me whose prints these are.' I took a deep breath and told him about Richard and why he had would have pushed Bridge to her death. Sergeant Miller listened intently with questioning eyes. After I finished describing the series of events as I saw them he rubbed his chin for a few seconds. Eventually he spoke up.

'Well, that's just a theory, nothing more. Still, whatever happened, we need to question this young man. The very fact that he hasn't come forward to tell us that he was with Bridget just before her death is suspicious. We're going to sort out a search warrant right now, which will take a few hours. As soon as that's done we'll head round to his place. In the meantime, you go home and, Steve, don't you even *think* about visiting Mr Stimp now, OK?' Miller was staring at me with his unflinching gaze and pointing his finger at me for emphasis as he said the last words.

I agreed and stood up.

I knew exactly where I was headed before I'd even left the police station.

I asked the cab driver to drop me off round the corner from where he lived. I wanted to review my strategy and I certainly didn't want him to see me arrive. I paid the driver, who'd been telling me all the way about his novel theory that there were too many immigrants in London, and walked towards Richard's door. I still didn't have a strategy by the time I arrived there but I was too angry to sit around forming one. I'd shoot from the hip and ask questions later. I knew that I was being irrational. I knew that what I intended to do might get me in serious trouble with the police, but this was no time for calm analysis. It was time for decisive action and to hell with the consequences.

I rang his bell and after a few nervous moments he answered. My heart rate immediately went up a notch. I had to play it cool, but I was seething. This fucker had killed my girl.

'Hi, Richard, it's Steve. I've been thinking about your offer and I'm in. I know those fuckers are grassing me up so I've got no choice but to return the favour . . . but only if you can promise me that my cooperation is taken into account by any investigation, OK?' It took all of my acting abilities to appear calm and humble.

Richard could barely control his glee. I could sense his joy through the intercom. He blurted out 'Come up to the third floor' and buzzed me in within a second – as if he were worried that I might change my mind at any moment. I grimly pushed the door open and climbed the stairs, my anger rising with each step. By the time I'd reached the third floor I was like a coiled spring.

When I got to his door it was already open and Richard was standing by it, a triumphant smile glued to his smug face. I walked up to him sheepishly, as seemed appropriate, and then lamped him as hard as I could on the nose. He flew back into his front room and I immediately followed him in, shaking my poor bruised knuckles. It was the first time I'd punched someone in the face for over a decade and I'd forgotten just how painful it could be.

Richard was on his back scrabbling away from me, a look of utter horror on his face. I slammed the door shut behind me and jumped on him, pinning his arms to the ground. Since he was a skinny runt who had probably never seen the inside of a gym, this didn't prove too hard. I found myself sitting on Richard's stomach with both his wrists pinned to the floor by the side of his head – a position that wouldn't have looked out of place in a school playground.

'OK, you little shit. I want answers and I want them now. I know you were with Bridget when she died and I've told the police. Your fingerprints have been found in her flat and you're going to get nicked. But if you don't tell me exactly what happened they're gonna need a fucking ambulance to take you out of here, OK?' I spat out each word. Richard was squirming like an eel, his eyes wide with fear. Eventually he stopped struggling, closed his eyes and began to speak, his pathetic high-pitched voice causing my hackles to rise even further.

'All right, all right . . . I did go round to see her on Sunday afternoon, just before she died. I wanted to tell her that I'd had nothing to do with her being fired. I'd been unable to sleep all weekend worrying about it. Anyway, she opened the door and she was in a terrible state. She was wearing some stained T-shirt and nothing else. I couldn't bear to see that beautiful woman degrade herself like that. At first she didn't even recognise me, she was so out of it. I went in there and tried to explain that her dismissal was not my doing. She sat me down and kept offering me booze and I had a couple of glasses. Anyway, once she'd worked out who I was, she started going a bit mad. She was snorting cocaine and knocking back champagne. I pleaded with her to stop but she just laughed at me. Suddenly, for no reason, she flew into an uncontrollable rage and threw me out.'

There was a long pause. Richard took a deep breath and said: 'Look, I swear that's how it happened. I never told the police because . . . well, I didn't want to be associated with that druggie scene. There'd be all sorts of awkward questions . . .' There was something very genuine about the way Richard recounted the story and there were too many details that tallied with what I already knew. Only a truly masterful liar could have pulled the wool over my eyes on this one and that was one thing Richard was not. I felt my body go limp and my grip on Richard's wrists loosen.

'You've always fancied her, haven't you?' I said, a calmer tone to my voice. I asked the question almost as a friend . . . a friend who was painfully aware that they both suffered from the same debilitating malady.

'Yeah, I've always loved Bridget . . . and I know you have too. It was written all over your face whenever you two were together.' I felt myself well up. The sudden remembrance of how much I missed her was proving too much. I desperately tried to stop the tears but I couldn't. I found myself in the undignified situation of sitting on a man's stomach with tears rolling down my face and on to his.

After a few seconds I pulled myself together. I stood up and walked towards the front door, my head bowed. Just as I reached the door, Richard, who was now sitting upright, spoke up.

'You know who you should really be questioning, don't you?'

I turned round and said wearily, 'No. Who's that?'

'Your mate Fergus.'

'Oh, fuck off, Richard. Why don't you leave it, OK? You don't need to turn us against each other – we've already done that ourselves.'

'No, I'm serious. You know that I've been investigating all of you, trying to get evidence that you were involved in the Geldlust affair? Well, it turns out that out of all of you, Fergus is the wild card. That guy is a nutter. Ever wondered why he left the army after only nine months? Well, I'll tell you. He was dismissed for violent behaviour. Apparently, two guys on the parade ground were taking the piss out of him and he just lost it. He smashed their heads around with his rifle butt. He had to be pulled off or he could have killed them. I'm telling you, the guy is a headcase. He might easily have killed Bridget. He's the one you should be questioning.'

I stared at Richard and tried to compute this new information. It was almost certainly true, because Richard knew I could check up on it. I'd also seen Fergus in action myself with those hicks down in Australia, and it wasn't a pretty sight. There was no doubt he had a short fuse. But there was also no doubt that he loved Bridget and wouldn't touch a hair on her head. I wasn't going to take any more of Richard's bullshit.

'Listen, Richard, Fergus might have a temper but he loved Bridge to bits. There's no way he'd hurt her, OK? And by the way, don't you dare tell the guys who are coming here about your pathetic little theory.' I couldn't wait for his next question.

'What guys?'

'Oh, the big uniformed guys who are gonna be here in about an hour,' I sneered. And with that I marched out, closing the door behind me.

There was just one last person I needed to talk to and it wasn't going to be much fun at all.

Twenty-Seven

The Golden Eagle pub, Notting Hill Gate
Saturday, 18 December, 2.45 p.m.

RACHEL WALKED INTO THE PUB in her usual tentative manner. She looked around and smiled awkwardly when she saw me seated with a pint. I smiled back, stood up and gave her a big bear hug. She was probably wondering why I held on to her for several seconds longer than normal. I kissed her cheeks and then went to the bar and bought her a vodka and Slimline tonic because, as she'd explained on the phone, she was on yet another diet. Since I'd known her she'd always been on some kind of diet and yet her weight never seemed to change. As soon as we were both seated she started babbling on about Darren and the kids and how a divorce looked likely. I listened to her for a while but then couldn't bear to hear any more about her domestic trials. I had no choice but to interrupt her. I looked her straight in the eyes, held my hand up and said, 'Rachel, please, please, stop. I've got something I have to tell you . . . something awful.' She stared at me. I took a deep breath and came out with it. 'I'm so sorry, but . . . but Colum's dead.'

Rachel's mouth dropped. Her eyes widened in disbelief.

'What? What? How? When?' I could see she was holding back tears.

'Thursday night. He was mugged and his head hit the tarmac and he died. I know . . . I can't bear it. He called me. He was about to tell me something when he was attacked. I heard him struggling to hold on . . .'

Rachel continued staring at me for a few seconds and then dropped her head into her hands and began to sob. I went and sat next to her and put my arm around her shoulders. I rocked her gently back and forth.

'I know, I know . . . it's fucking terrible. We met for a game of pool just before he died and he told me about you two. He told me . . . in a roundabout way . . . that he loved you. I'm so sorry, I'm so sorry.'

Rachel's sobbing went into overdrive. I offered her a tissue but she just kept her head in her hands. Some of the pub's other customers stared at us until I glared back at them. I held her in my arms, gently rocking her back and forth, for what seemed like hours. Eventually she pulled herself together and looked up. Her eyes were bright red and her cheeks were puffy. I continued to hold her as she tried to speak. At first it was difficult to hear her through the sobs, but then the words became clearer.

'I just can't bear this. First Bridge and now Colum. What the fuck is going on?'

'I know. It's awful. Unbearable. Why is this happening to us?'

'And I'm completely racked with guilt, I can't tell you. You know Bridge kept calling me the weekend she died and I never answered her calls. I should have been there for her . . . I could have stopped her . . .' Her voice tailed off but we both knew she had been about to say 'killing herself'.

'Look, I really want to find out what happened that morning . . . what was going on at Bridge's flat. I want to ask you just one question.' I had decided before this meeting that I wouldn't tell Rachel about the figure seen in Bridget's room.

'OK, what is it?'

'Tell me what Bridge said about her and Fergus. You were supposed to be her best mate. She must have told you how things were going for them and I need to know.'

Rachel looked quizzical. She paused, took a few deep breaths and then spoke. 'Bridge and Fergus were having major problems. Fergus is a control freak and he could be quite abusive. She showed me some nasty bruises where he hit her just a few days before she died. Look, out of respect for Fergus, I haven't told anyone this, but Bridget was going to end it and he knew she was.'

'What the fuck? I thought everything was tickety-boo? Fergus told me that they'd just got engaged!'

I couldn't believe what I was hearing. Why hadn't

Bridget told me the truth? Who was she protecting? Me? Fergus? What was she hiding? Before I could answer my own questions Rachel said angrily: 'That's bullshit. It's true that Fergus asked her to marry him about a week before she died but she hadn't said yes. She'd basically said "let me think about it" and she only did that because she was so worried that he'd beat the crap out of her if she told him the truth. She planned to leave him.' Rachel looked into my eyes for several seconds and with a strange smile added sadly, 'I know this sounds crazy . . . but I think she might still have held a candle for you.'

It was my turn to burst into tears. Christ alive, I hadn't just lost a friend . . . I might just have lost my soul partner. The loneliness that had sucked me dry for most of the last fifteen years need never have blighted my life. I could have been happy. I could have had a real life. Before I could dwell too long on the horrifying implications of Rachel's throw-away comment, she continued: 'Look, Steve, if you don't believe me about what Fergus is like, call her mum up. She knew exactly what was going on. Bridge had confided in her. I've got her number.'

I remembered how cold Bridget's mum had been to Fergus on the day of the funeral. I remembered her refusing to hug Fergus after it. Without a second's pause I took the number from Rachel and excused myself. I walked outside the pub into the crisp, cool winter's day. Late Christmas shoppers buying presents for their loved ones thronged the street, reminding me once again of what I'd lost. I dialled

Diane Von Blixen's mobile, and she answered after a few rings. After the initial pleasantries I got to the point.

'Look, Mrs Von Blixen, I want to ask you a question. It's something that's been playing on my mind and I hope you can help me. I'm sorry if this is raking over painful ground, but could you please tell me what you really thought about Fergus and Bridget's relationship?'

She didn't pause. There was fury in her voice. 'That man was a monster and he hit my little baby . . . but what drove him really mad is what Bridget did just before she died.' There was a long pause; it sounded as if Diane was crying. At last she managed to speak. 'I can hardly bring myself to say this, but . . . she aborted his baby the week before she died . . . and I think he might have found out about it.'

I gulped once, then twice. My innards tied themselves in knots. Now it really did make sense. Bridget hadn't been drinking or doing coke in the weeks before her death because she was pregnant. She'd taken the early part of her final week off sick because she'd had an abortion. Oh my dear God! What the fuck would Fergus do if he found out that his supposed wife-to-be had aborted his baby? What would that do to a man with such a short fuse? What would that violent bastard do if he then went round to her flat and she, out of her face, told him that it was over between them?

The answer was obvious.

He'd kill her.

Twenty-Eight

The Coach and Horses pub, the Embankment
Sunday, 19 December, 12.35 p.m.

I CALLED FERGUS ON SATURDAY night to tell him it was
time we had a 'nice Sunday pub lunch' together. Now
that I'd processed all the information I'd garnered over
the previous days it was crystal clear that my supposedly best
friend was a psycho. All the jigsaw pieces finally fitted
perfectly into place. The fucker had knocked around the
woman I could have spent the rest of my life with and had
pushed her out of a window because his fragile ego couldn't
cope with the fact she didn't want to marry him. He had
obviously found out she was going to end it and that she'd
aborted his child and his raging anger had got the better of
him. He must have lost it when he'd gone round to see her
that Monday morning and pushed her out of that window. It
must have been him all along who'd been following Bridge in
the scarf and hat, stalking her like a crazed lunatic, trying to

find out if she was having an affair with me or anyone else. Well, I had a plan. I would get the fucker to confess and then I'd get Sergeant Miller to come over and arrest him. I'd been formulating the plan all night and it was a sure-fire winner.

I waited at the corner table supping my pint and frantically tapping my foot on the floor. I'd arrived half an hour early for the meeting and had been getting increasingly nervous with each passing minute. I was about to confront someone I'd shared many of the best moments of my life with. This was the guy I'd first smoked pot with, the guy I'd chased girls with at school, the guy I'd relied on when I was in trouble. We'd hardly ever raised our voices to each other and I'd lost count of the times we'd got drunk and partied. Bonding moments from Ibiza to Miami, from Goa to Sydney. But who the fuck was he really? Did I know him at all? Whoever he was, he'd destroyed everything that had meant anything to me. He'd taken Bridget's life . . . and he'd ruined mine.

After another pint, I saw a tall, broad figure through the frosted glass approaching the pub's front door. I knew it was Fergus even before he'd opened it. His strong, confident walk was unmistakable, but whereas before I'd thought of it as a sign of his solid self-assurance, I now viewed it as the egotistical swagger of a wife beater. He came in with a curious smile on his face. I didn't return the favour. If my upcoming act was to be convincing this was no time for false bonhomie. I felt like killing the bastard anyway so it wasn't hard being frosty. His step slowed a little as he approached my table. I could tell that he'd immediately sensed that something was up.

'Hello, mate. How's it going?' His tone was unusually tentative.

'Hi, Fergus. Not too bad, I suppose.'

'Do you want a pint?'

'No, I'm fine, thanks.'

'Erm . . . I'll just get one and join you, then.' The formality of this encounter was something that neither of us had experienced before. If this didn't put him on the back foot then nothing would. He returned with his pint and sat down opposite me. I stared at him for a few seconds. He stared back. Eventually, he broke the silence.

'So, something's obviously on your mind.'

I continued staring at him. 'Yep, something is most definitely on my mind.' Another long pause.

'So, are you going to tell me?'

I didn't say a word. I simply pulled out an orange envelope from the breast pocket of my overcoat and placed it face down on the table in front of me. The lilac letter inside just peeked out. I went on staring at Fergus. He looked down and then raised his head and looked back at me.

'What's that?'

'You know exactly what that is. It's a letter from Bridget. She sent it to me two days before she died but the silly bint was in such a state she posted it to my old address and the new owners have only just forwarded it on to me.' In fact, I'd bought the orange envelope and lilac paper from Rymans the day before, because Bridget wrote all her personal letters using that combination.

'Let me see it,' Fergus said, his hand darting out towards the letter. I pulled it straight into my lap. I could see he was beginning to get angry. The glare in his eyes intensified. I'd seen that expression a few times before. It looked as though he might jump over the table and grab the letter off me at any moment.

'There's no need for you to see it. I can tell you what it says.'

'OK, fucking *tell* me then.' He spat the words out. His temper was beginning to show itself. It didn't use to scare me but it did now that I knew what he was capable of. I felt my heart rate go up a notch. Whatever happened I had to stay calm.

'All right, but you're not gonna like what it says.'

'Just fucking *get* on with it.' I could see his body tensing up. He really was seething now. Good. I wanted him to be irrational – that way he'd be easier to manipulate.

'OK, Bridget wrote this letter to me out of desperation . . . as if she were scared you might do something stupid and she wanted to leave some evidence for me. She describes in great detail how abusive you've been to her – how you hit her and threatened her.' I could see Fergus wince when I said those last words. Maybe I'd over-egged it a bit.

'She also goes on to say that you weren't engaged. In fact, she'd effectively said no but was too scared to tell you straight up. In actual fact, she was desperate to end it with you but she knew you'd go mental if she did because you're such a fucking control freak.'

I allowed the last words to sink in before I came out with the *coup de grâce*. 'Finally, she tells me that she'd got rid of your baby and she thought that you might have found out about it because she'd realised that it was you who had been following her around in a scarf and hat . . . just like you've been following the rest of us around. That time she caught John was a one-off. She knew you had it in you to kill her and that's why she wrote this letter to me. She was scared and I . . . I didn't protect her.' My voice tailed off. Fergus was staring right through me. He'd got the Vietnam vet 2,000-yard stare. He wasn't blinking. It was as if he'd entered a catatonic state – David Blaine on Mogadon. I went on.

'I also know that you got kicked out of the army for battering two lads with your rifle. Finally, I have recently been informed by the police that a man fitting your description was in her room when she died. Fergus . . .' I took another deep breath. 'Fergus, I know you killed Bridget. You're a *fucking* murderer and I'm going to the police right now.' I slammed my hand on the table, the case for the prosecution complete.

Fergus's face didn't betray any emotion. He just kept staring straight through me. His mind was clearly somewhere else. Then, slowly, he returned to earth. His eyes connected with mine. After about a minute he started shaking his head slowly from side to side. I couldn't believe it; the prick had a wry smile on his face. He dropped his head but continued shaking it. I could tell there were tears flowing down his cheeks. A few of them dropped on to the table. I knew then that I was right. He hadn't appeared shocked at any of my revelations, even the ones I'd surmised, which meant they must have been true. His silence condemned him just as surely as his tears did. After another thirty seconds of shoe gazing, he spoke up.

'Well, you are right about one thing.' He paused. 'I am a murderer.'

'I knew it, you wanker. You killed Bridget, *my* Bridge. I'm calling the police right now.' A triumphant smile spread across my face. I ceremoniously took out my mobile ready to call Sergeant Miller. But Fergus wasn't finished.

'Mate, you've got it all wrong. The only person I killed was Colum and that was unintentional. No, my friend, I didn't kill Bridget . . .' There was a long pause. I couldn't believe what I was hearing. Before I could process this new piece of information about Colum, Fergus leaned forward and pointed his finger at me. 'I didn't kill Bridget. I loved that girl with all my heart.' Fergus took a deep breath. 'But you lot did and that's why you all had to be punished . . . and punished in the right way.'

I leant back in my seat, my frazzled mind flitting in every possible direction. What the hell was he talking about? Why would any of us have harmed her? How could we all have killed her? What did he mean 'punished in the right way'?

* * *

'So, after we played squash Colum came right out with it. He'd been wanting to tell us both for weeks but couldn't bring himself to do it. But the guilt was eating him up and after a few lines he started talking. He was there when Bridge fell . . . well, in body, if not in spirit, so he said. He'd been getting high on crystal meth and ketamine and he told me that when Bridge fell he was in a catatonic state. It was just her scream that woke him out of his stupor. When he realised that she'd fallen he panicked and just upped and left. He couldn't be dealing with the police when he was that high and with all those drugs around.' Fergus was speaking quietly and steadily so that only I would hear his words. I was completely dumbstruck. I could do nothing but go on listening.

'What he told me didn't surprise me. I'd always suspected that fat fuck had been with her that weekend . . . getting her high on John's drugs . . . probably trying to get into her knickers, the sleazy cunt. After he told me, I tried to keep calm. I even let him go and shook his hand but once back inside my flat I felt the anger rising. That fucker as good as killed my Bridget. He may not have pushed her, but he'd got her high and he didn't stop her. So I ran after him and got to him just before he'd arrived home. I don't know what I was thinking. I was seeing red. I ran up to him from behind and before he could turn round jumped and brought my elbow smashing down on the back of his neck. He fell like a sack of potatoes. After a few kicks I realised he was in a bad way . . . I thought he was knocked out but I didn't think he was dead. I just grabbed his wallet to make it look like a mugging and pissed off. You must have arrived just minutes after I left.'

'Christ! You killed Colum. You fucking killed Colum!' I couldn't believe what I was hearing.

'I did . . . but I didn't mean to and I only half regret it. I'd already punished him for his role in bringing about Bridge's death before I'd found out for sure that he had been with her at the end by getting the FSA to raid his firm. But the fact that I killed him seems appropriate because, as far as I'm concerned,' he said, jabbing his finger into his own chest, 'he did kill Bridget. The punishment should fit the crime, an eye for an eye and all that. And let's not forget that fat tosser was probably going to dob us all in. You caught him talking to the police . . . and although he told me after one squash game that he had been merely "discussing his options" and hadn't told them a thing, who knows with that lying prick?'

There was a slightly mad glare in Fergus's eyes but there was a twisted logic to what he was saying. I looked away, my mind racing at a thousand miles an hour. After a few seconds I turned back to Fergus and spoke in as slow and deliberate a fashion as I could – working out what I was saying as I said it.

'The punishment should fit the crime, eh? So, you knew that John sold Bridget the drugs she took so you told the police about his secret stash and got the police to raid him, right?'

'Right. And I immediately told Richard about John's drugs bust, and about Colum's raid . . . admittedly with a pencil in my mouth so he didn't know who I was.'

'And Rachel?'

'Well, Rachel, her supposed best mate, hadn't been there to support her in her hour of need so I took away her "support" . . . her family . . . by taking those photos of her with Colum and sending them to Darren knowing they'd probably split up.'

'And me . . . OK, it was you outside my flat that night trying to freak me out . . . but why the fuck did you tell Richard about the Black Cat? Why did you want to get at me?'

He seemed to ignore my question at first. After a few seconds he lent in and said, 'Listen, I admit Bridget was getting a bit confused about us towards the end, but we were still solid.' The delusional idiot probably believed what he was saying. 'The abortion, the not saying yes immediately to my proposal . . . there could only have been one explanation for that . . . and that's you. You were getting her high and making a play for her. You were turning her against me. Look at how you told the police she was your bird. How fucking dare you! You wanted to rekindle your romance, so I thought I'd remind you and your loved ones just how "romantic" you are – you whoring little fucker.' Fergus had a disgusted sneer on his face as he spat out the words.

'That's fucking lies!' I shouted, feeling my face flush red with anger. 'I've always liked Bridge but while she was your girl I wasn't going to do a damn thing. I had my chance fifteen years ago and I blew it.' I raised my hands heavenward. 'Christ alive, you've gone properly mad. You've fucked us all because of your pathetic delusions!' I was almost laughing at the horror of it all. But then I remembered something that didn't tally with his story. 'But I don't understand . . . someone was blackmailing you. Who was that?'

'I sent that note to myself to put everyone off the scent. If Rachel hadn't fortuitously decided to come round my house at the hour that the letter was due to arrive I was going to call you and have you be there for when it came.' There was a smug satisfaction in Fergus's explanation. Suddenly, I thought of another glaring discrepancy in his story.

'But . . . but what about Operation Grizzly? That was your baby and by fucking us up there was no way it was going to happen.'

'Mate, *wake up!* Smell the *fucking* coffee! There never was any Operation Grizzly – it was just another ruse to make me seem the innocent one. Once Yogi had been completed and I'd made my money it was all about getting revenge on you fuckers. Grizzly was just a smokescreen so no one suspected me.'

'You smug prick! Your "revenge" has fucked up any chance that we're gonna get our hands on the winnings that Colum's fund made – that's millions of pounds that had been earmarked for all of us, including you. Yeah, and despite Colum's death, thanks to you, there's still a chance the FSA are going to find out that we organised the bear raid. We might all go to fucking jail.'

'Correction, my friend. You lot might go to jail. Let's look at who did what. You spread a computer virus at your bank, Rachel started a bogus FSA investigation, John convinced his colleagues to sell all their Geldlust shares, Colum got his fund to short Geldlust in every conceivable way . . . and all these acts were perfectly coordinated. They are detectable crimes. I was just a dumb schmuck who got conned by his so-called friends into writing the relevant articles that would further their money-making schemes. In fact, I'm the only one of us who didn't get his fingers dirty . . . so if any of you are thinking of going to the police about Colum I'd most definitely think again.'

I couldn't speak. The scumbag had every angle covered and he knew it. Before I could protest he was speaking again.

'Oh yeah, and I'm not too bothered about not getting any money from Colum's fund. You have no idea how many people I got to short Geldlust and I'm not talking first cousins or anyone closely connected to me, unlike you gormless dicks. No, I've got over thirty people with no traceable connection to me who have together made me millions.' Fergus sat back, nodding his head. It was as if he was willing me to find a flaw in his strategy. I couldn't.

I took a sip of my beer. My hand was visibly shaking. This was game, set and match to Fergus. There was nothing I could do. My shoulders slumped and I stared at the table. I took a few deep breaths as I tried to find a flaw in his scheme. There were none. After another long pause I spoke up.

'So, what are you going to do now? How are you going to spend all your ill-gotten gains?'

'Oh, I know *exactly* what I'm going to do. I'm going to the tropics and I'm going to set up a commune. I'm going to show the world that there is an alternative to capitalism. You may think I'm just some daft pinko but I'm not. I'm going to shake up the *fucking* world!' Fergus was slamming his fist on the table. Several people on the tables near us turned round to see what the fuss was about. I looked at the insane glare in Fergus's eyes and realised then that he had lost it. Bridget's death had sent my old friend over the edge and there was no coming back. The madman was on a mission. He'd lost the love of his life and put all his boundless energy into 'shaking up the world' . . . whatever that meant.

And with that Fergus stood up. He held his hand out and after a reluctant pause I shook it. I knew I'd probably never see him again. I'd lost the love of my life and my best friend in the space of a month. Fergus turned towards the exit and started walking away from me. Then he stopped dead in his tracks and turned round.

'There is one other thing you should know. Colum told me that Bridge had been dancing on that windowsill all night off and on before she fell. She never killed herself. She just got high and slipped in the rain. It was just . . . just one of those things . . .' Fergus's voice tailed off. I could see that he was holding back the tears. He walked away before I could say anything. I watched him leave and despair took hold of my soul. We might have had our revenge on Geldlust for Bridget's dismissal and made a few quid but none of the other things should have happened: Colum's death, John's upcoming trial, Rachel's imminent divorce and my potential humiliation should Richard go public had all been for nothing. None of it had to happen. This whole thing had just been an accident.

A pointless joke by the gods on six people who used to be friends.

Epilogue

Kensal Green Cemetery
Wednesday, 22 December, 11.30 a.m.

I SUPPOSE THE HOLE COLUM Boyd was being lowered into at 11.30 a.m. on that grey December morning was the only one on this planet that he wouldn't have been happy to enter when alive.

His funeral was a tragic affair. Both Colum's parents had died years before, and he had very few genuine pals. The employees from Alpha Max had come to 'pay their respects' but they weren't his real friends – just a bunch of guys hoping that the FSA investigation into their firm wouldn't discover anything that would jeopardise their upcoming bonuses. They were slimy little scumbags and they left as soon as the ceremony was over. His only 'friends' in attendance were me, John and Rachel and only one of us genuinely liked him whilst he was alive. Not surprisingly, Fergus didn't turn up. I didn't tell the others what he'd done. There seemed no point, and if Rachel had got all emotional and told the police about Colum's murder, as seemed likely, then we'd all have been in big trouble. I told them that it had all been too much for Fergus and that he was jibbing out. I added that he was going to take a long holiday and that I suspected it would be some time before we saw him again.

After the vicar had done his bit the three of us trudged through the rain to the William IV and sat there, once again having just buried another of our gang. On the walk to the pub no one said a damn thing. Once we'd found a table, I bought three pints and settled down for yet more awkward silence. I decided to say something before we were mistaken for a convention of Trappist monks.

'Listen, John, I just want to say sorry about the other day. I never really thought you were the snitch. It's just that Fergus and I had agreed that I should bluff you just to make sure. We were pretty damn sure that it was Colum . . . so no hard feelings, OK?'

'Yeah, that's OK. Everything got so fucked up that no one knew what to believe any more.'

'But aren't you going to get fired today unless you tell Richard everything you know about Yogi?' asked Rachel, appearing genuinely concerned. She'd always been rather maternal towards John, who both resented and enjoyed her motherly attention.

'Yeah, but . . . that's the way it goes. I'm not going to say anything to Richard about Yogi and so he'll tell my boss about the bust and I'll get fired. Still, even without Colum's money, I'm still due to make over a hundred grand from my friends and family who took a bet on Geldlust's demise. That's better than a poke in the eye with a sharp stick!' John was definitely becoming more confident. This whole shit storm seemed to have brought him out of his shell. Rachel had told me earlier that he'd given up the Class A and it seemed to be working for him.

'Well, do you still want your job? Because if you do, then I think we can persuade Richard not to tell your firm about the drugs bust. Hell, we could get him to stop trying to get us all nicked. Believe me, the little twat's just as corrupt as the rest of us. Money talks and bullshit walks. Let's call him right now and make him an offer he can't refuse. All we have to do is agree the amount we're willing to offer him to scupper Geldlust's investigation into Yogi. Those gormless pinheads are treating him like a member of their team in their investigation so he can definitely help us. Whaddya reckon?' I looked at my both my partners in crime, willing them to agree with me.

I wasn't being entirely honest with John and Rachel. In reality, I'd met up with Richard the day before. He'd managed to explain his presence at Bridget's flat to the police and, although they had not 'eliminated him from their inquiries', he was a free man. I'd gone round to his flat and, whilst not admitting we'd brought Geldlust down, told him that we were willing to pay him quite a lot of money to ensure he did everything he could to sabotage the FSA investigation. He'd told me a cool two hundred grand should just about cover it and I'd replied that that would be no problem provided it also bought his silence re John's drug bust. The crooked little prick hardly needed any persuasion. I could virtually see dollar signs in his beady little eyes.

I asked Rachel and John how much we were willing to pay to get Richard off our back and steered them to £200,000. I then took my mobile out and walked out of the pub. After about ten minutes I sauntered back in with a smile on my face pretending to have called Richard. When they heard of my 'success', we all toasted man's inherently corrupt nature, which had almost certainly just saved our hairy arses from prison.

It was after that cynical toast that Rachel asked the question that had been playing on all our minds.

'But why . . . why do you think we did it? It was such a mad thing to do. What really made us do it?' she asked with her usual wide-eyed innocence.

John and I thought for a second and then both blurted out our answers simultaneously: 'Greed,' I said. 'Revenge,' said John. We looked at each other and smiled. Then I said much more quietly, 'Love,' thinking of Bridge. John replied, 'Hate,' almost certainly thinking of the banks. Finally, we said in unison, 'For the fuck of it!'

Rachel looked at us both and let out a little laugh. 'Maybe we should have worked out why we were doing it beforehand, eh? Well, whatever our reasons we certainly shook things up a bit there, didn't we?'

We all clinked our glasses again. We'd made some cash and had shaken things up a bit but we all knew that the thing we'd shaken up most was our gang. Things would never be the same again for any of us.

I finished my pint and looked at my two old friends. There was only one thing left to say.

'One for the road?'

'Yeah, and one for the ones we never rode!'

And for a brief moment everything seemed all right.

I had another leprechaun dream last night. This time he was a happy little feller – not the skull-faced monstrosity from before. He took me by the hand and we leapt straight into the air. We flew over London and headed west. We soon arrived at the coast but we kept on flying. Occasionally I'd look at the leprechaun and he'd squeeze my hand and give me a reassuring smile back. Suddenly, we came to a beautiful tropical island, covered in thick jungle and surrounded by turquoise lagoons. We started dropping and before long I could see a clearing in the palm trees with a little village of wooden huts at its centre. We landed on the soft, lush grass and walked hand in hand towards a bronzed man sitting on a wicker chair. The sun beat on my back. A gentle breeze cooled my face. The man wore nothing but a loincloth. Naked, laughing children were playing around him. As we got nearer I could see that it was Fergus. He smiled, stood up and walked towards me with open arms. He was about to hug me when I suddenly woke up. I wiped my eyes feeling happier than I had for many, many years.

I knew then that I hadn't seen the last of Fergus. I knew then that I'd see him again . . . and sooner rather than later.

Just Business

Geraint Anderson

IT'S MURDER IN THE CITY . . .

The bestselling author of CITYBOY returns with an explosive, edge-of-the-seat thriller of City corruption, devious scams and monstrously bad behaviour.

Steve Jones, our Cityboy hero, wants to get out of the city. But he needs a big pay day. And, like the expert chancer he is, he sees an opportunity.

Hacking into his boss's computer, he finds something that chills him to the bone.

But when his recklessness leads to murder and he becomes the prime suspect, it's time to go on the run. Together with his feisty on-off girlfriend Gemma, he improvises ingenious ways of outwitting the authorities, MI5 and a vicious drug cartel's highly trained killers. It's a chase that forces Steve and Gemma halfway round the world in a desperate attempt to survive.

Praise for *Just Business*:

'Anderson has turned thriller writer to wreak yet more revenge on avarice. Cool plotting, smart polemic' *Mirror*

'As bold and innovative as its author, *Just Business* takes the reader on a breathtaking guided tour of cocaine blizzards, bankers' drafts, and emotional whirlwinds. I could put it down but not until long after I'd finished it. It's first class' Howard Marks

978 0 7553 8173 9

headline

Dr. Yes

Bateman

You don't say no to Dr. Yes, the charismatic plastic surgeon on the fast track to fame and fortune. But when the wife of obscure and paranoid crime writer Augustine Wogan disappears shortly after entering his exclusive clinic, Mystery Man, the Small Bookseller with No Name, is persuaded to investigate.

Business is in the doldrums for No Alibis, Mystery Man's infamous crime bookshop. And, as fatherhood approaches, our intrepid hero is interested only in a quick buck and the chance to exploit a neglected writer. But he soon finds himself up to his neck in murder, make-up and madness – and face to face with the most gruesome serial killer . . . since the last one.

Bateman: the word on the street:

'I've been a fan of Colin Bateman ever since his first crime novel and he just seems to get better and better' Ian Rankin

'Bateman has a truly unique voice . . . he is a dark and brilliant champion of words' James Nesbitt

'Sometimes brutal, often blackly humorous and always terrific' *Observer*

978 0 7553 7861 6

headline

Shadow Force

Matt Lynn

AN UNDERCOVER OPERATION.
A TOP SECRET UNIT.
A DEATH SENTENCE FOR DEATH FORCE?

It's a mission no sane fighter would willingly accept. But what if there was no choice?

Somali-based pirates are attacking ships off the coast of Africa, demanding tens of millions of dollars in ransoms.

The elite fighting men from Death Inc are thrown into action in their most dangerous mission yet. They are the British government's Shadow Force: a top-secret unit, sent into Somalia to destroy the pirates.

But it soon becomes clear they have been lured into a deadly conspiracy, in which only they are expendable . . .

And the battle begins . . .

Praise for Matt Lynn:

'A cracking action thriller. You can taste the dust and smell the blood' *Daily Express*

'Matt Lynn's novel is up there with the finest that Andy McNab or Chris Ryan have ever penned' *News of the World*

978 0 7553 7170 9

headline

Cityboy: Beer and Loathing in the Square Mile

Geraint Anderson

In this no-holds-barred, warts-and-all account of life in London's financial heartland, Cityboy breaks the Square Mile's code of silence, revealing tricks of the trade and the corrupt, murky underbelly at the heart of life in the City. Drawing on his experience as a young analyst in a major investment bank, the six-figure bonuses, monstrous egos, and the everyday culture of verbal and substance abuse that fuels the world's money markets is brutally exposed as Cityboy describes his ascent up the hierarchy of this intensely competitive and morally dubious industry, and how it almost cost him his sanity.

'Engaging, timely and important' *The Times*

'His timing couldn't be better . . . London's pernicious financial world reveals itself in all its ugliness' *Daily Mail*

'As a primer to back-stabbing, bullying, drug-taking, gambling, boozing, lap-dancing, this takes some beating . . . a necessary and valuable book' *Evening Standard*

978 0 7553 4618 9

headline

Now you can buy any of these other bestselling
titles from your bookshop or
direct from the publisher.

FREE P&P AND UK DELIVERY
(Overseas and Ireland £3.50 per book)

Cityboy: Beer and Loathing in the Square Mile	Geraint Anderson	£8.99
Just Business	Geraint Anderson	£7.99
Plugged	Eoin Colfer	£6.99
Dr. Yes	Bateman	£8.99
Shadow Force	Matt Lynn	£7.99
If It Bleeds	Duncan Campbell	£7.99
Buried Secrets	Joseph Finder	£6.99
The Gods of Atlantis	David Gibbins	£6.99
Satori	Trevanian	£6.99

TO ORDER SIMPLY CALL THIS NUMBER

01235 400 414

or visit our website: www.headline.co.uk